Also by ANTHONY BAILEY

In the Village

In the Village

Anthony Bailey

Alfred A. Knopf   New York
1971

To
JOHN *and* MARY UPDIKE

In a few places in this account I have changed names, tenses, and details.

—A. B.

*Man is matter transforming
itself into the ideal.*

—Nicholas Ogarev

In the Village

1

THERE ARE TWO OR THREE walkers in the village, but Frankie Keane is the one I generally pass at night. Frank is the middle-aged bachelor who runs the newspaper shop, Keane's News Office (a name correctly suggesting a place where news is retailed not only in printed form), and halfway along Water Street on a frosty December evening I meet Frank and his poodle, stepping quickly along. "How is it down your end?" says Frank, making it seem we have come a long way to this momentary encounter. "Fine," I say, "and yours?" "Great," says Frank. We walk past each other, heading on. Similarly, coming the other way down Main Street on the first balmy night in June are Frank and his dog. "Lovely night, Frank," I say, opening the proceedings. He replies: "It is. Though a bit cold down your way still." And we pass. I appreciate Frank's subtle announcement of the lower temperature in my part of the village, the Point, which is barely a quarter of a mile from this spot "uptown." By midsummer chances have improved of finding more people out of doors, if not actually walking. On a sticky night in late July, after dinner, I find

In the Village

Frank chatting to the La Gruas, outside their appliance store on Water Street. Maurice La Grua is the town tax collector and photographer for school pictures, passports, and weddings. The store is one of the dozen, including Frank's, which make up the small commercial center of the place. From here, on this kind of night, still and hot, you can hear harbor sounds—the chatter of an outboard motor or a brief and perhaps accidental blast of a foghorn. The fog has lifted for the first time in three days, so that down in the parking lot on the Point, the tip of the peninsula on which the village stands, you can see as far as the Inner Breakwater or Wamphassuc Point on the other side of the harbor. Mosquitoes are out and about, biting. I wonder what has become of the mosquito-eating purple martins which were supposed to take up residence in the martin house, a many-storied, multiple martin-family dwelling set up by the Historical Society (whose members are not usually fond of apartment houses) on the old Lighthouse lawn.

My walk has taken me up Water Street, past the former Atwood Machine Works, now the Plax division of Monsanto, a big nineteenth-century brick factory building, past the Harbor View seafood restaurant, whose view is mostly of the Plax parking lot, past Bindloss's hardware store, and then past a stretch of houses, those on the left side being waterfront property, before reaching the stores: Ernie's Delicatessen, the Pin Money Shop (better second-hand and previously owned clothes, the four real-estate agents, the two antique shops, the three barber shops, the two liquor stores, the two grocery markets, Ed's Cleaning, The Lure (high-season sportswear and knickknacks), Cameron's Coffee Shop, and Stonington Department Store, which has one department, and is run by Mr. Eli Siegel and his wife. Paul Schepis, pronounced "Skeps," is the owner of the package store I frequent, and I go, as infrequently as I can since I hate having my hair cut, to Squadrito's Barber Shop. Mr. Squadrito, the third generation of Squadritos to run a barber shop in the village, is Mr. Schepis's brother-in-law. At the moment we seem to be favoring the Stonington Market, run by the Chiappones, more relations of Mr. Schepis, rather than Roland's Market, run by Roland Albamonte, though we used to go to Roland's and may yet return there.

I have reached Wadawanuck Square, which babysitters call the park. It is a square, formed by Water Street, Broad Street, Main Street, and High Street. In the middle sits the Stonington Free Library, a marble mausoleumlike structure, and paths reach out diagonally to the corners of the square through the grass, under the thick, high trees. On three sides the square is flanked by large frame houses, though there is a smattering of business: the Drug Store, the Stonington Craft Shop, and the Book Mart. The doctor's house sits on one corner and diagonally opposite it is the Culbert Palmer house, a huge Victorian horror which I covet, and in which the

Culbert Palmers (also of Fifth Avenue, Manhattan) dwell mainly in summer. I disapprove of this, even though I don't know them, and even though the houses of the village generally seem more real to me than their inhabitants: certainly the houses have been here longer than those who presently live in them. They are anchors, shelters, devices for incorporating people in a place. And for that reason, they need to be lived in. On the fourth side of the square is the post office and St. Mary's Catholic Church, both imitation colonial, though the post office is the less pretentious.

I continue down Water Street to the railroad tracks, where a barricade closes the old crossing. The one road from the village climbs over the track on a steel viaduct, which the village burgesses are always pestering the railroad authorities to keep in better condition than they in fact do. The railroad—formerly the New Haven shore line, now the bankrupt Penn Central—cuts across the broad neck of the peninsula, making it pretty much an island. As I walk along the weed-ridden gravel of the station parking lot, a passenger train comes through, the light shining out from the windows of the rocking parlor car, diner, and coaches, wheels rattling, diesel hammering, and the horn hooting already for the Wamphassuc crossing. Some of the windows are cracked by thrown rocks. The overheated wheels often throw out sparks, which in dry spring weather cause grass fires and keep the village firemen busy. The only train that stops

in the village now is a two-car Buddliner, New London
to Boston, 7:21 on weekday mornings. (It returns
from Providence at 6:20 in the evenings.) To get it
to stop you have to hold out your hand, demonstrating
that you are seriously intent on taking the train. In the
old lighthouse, now a museum, is the last ticket sold in
the Stonington station in 1949, a one-way from Stonington to Westerly (five miles away), presented by Billings
Fairbrother. (The old men who used to hang around the
station waiting room now, like Billings, hang out in a
more contemporary facility nearby, the lounge at Dodson's Boatyard, where cruising yachts—a private form
of transport—come in to moor for the night.) The "station" is now an open-fronted lean-to on the "up" or Boston side of the tracks, and there is very little to show
that the village was once the bustling terminus of the
New York and Stonington Railroad, which in 1832
received one of the first two railroad charters in Connecticut, giving it the right to run a line from Providence
to Stonington, where it would connect with steamboats
for New York. Major George Washington Whistler, the
painter's father, was assigned by the U.S. Army to sur-
vey the route. The first locomotive to pull a train into
the village was called the Roger Williams; the passenger
cars in those days were like stagecoaches with flanged
wheels. In fact, since there was no Episcopal church in
Stonington then, the Whistlers used to go to Westerly
every Sunday morning in a private railroad car, drawn

by horses. Grass fires then were started by the sparks from locomotive smokestacks rather than wheels or bearings. In the 1840's the steamers on which you could go overnight to New York City were called the *Oregon* and *Knickerbocker*. In 1889 the Thames River bridge was completed; because the trains no longer had to be ferried over, the steamers were doomed. The ferries had added only five minutes or so to the route (trains had to stop anyway for wood and water), but they added an excitement some passengers could have done without. Dickens wrote after making the trip from New York to Boston: "Two rivers have to be crossed and each time the whole train is banged aboard a big steamer. The steamer rises and falls with the river which the railroad don't do, and the train is banged up hill or banged down hill. In coming off the steamer at one of these crossings yesterday, we were banged up such a height that the rope broke and the carriage rushed back with a run down hill into the boat again. I whisked out in a moment, and two or three others after me, but nobody else seemed to care about it."

Now pedestrians can walk without much danger across the shore line, having casually looked for the *Patriot* or the *Merchants Limited*, or listened for the new Turbo-train, which because of the sharp bend in the tracks crawls through the village. The tracks were less of a division before the road viaduct was built and the footbridge was constructed at Elm Street. Despite the present feeling of separation, that section of the village has many large and prosperous Victorian houses—not at all wrong-side-of-the-track houses—together with the Town Hall and the new Community Center. The velvet mill is in this area too, though the auto dealers have deserted their premises there for new showrooms on Route One, the main Mystic-Westerly road.

The railroad, at any rate, is holding on longer than the interurban trolley. I walk for twenty yards or so along the old right-of-way, grassed over but scarcely more visible than a Celtic track or Bronze Age barrow. In this part of the state there was a Groton-Mystic-Stonington-Westerly trolley system, with connections to Norwich. For thirty years spanning the turn of the century, trams and trolleys in the northeast provided an excellent local public transportation service. Henry Ford did them in. I walk back under the viaduct—itself an act of tribute to the automobile and to drivers who don't want to stop and wait for a passing train—and swing back up Main Street, past the lumberyard and the Catholic parsonage. Here is another house I covet, a pure and simple two-story eighteenth-century white frame house belonging to Mrs. Stone, the novelist. Grace Stone was married to a naval man and spent years on the China station: she knows about gunboats, and was once shelled on the Yangtse River. I respectfully pass Henry Chapin's gambrel-roofed house, number 52, with a white chalk on white paint four-letter word just visible on a clapboard

under Henry's study window. The word has been there
for six years—I remember it there when we rented the
house during our first winter in the village. I admire
Henry's obstinacy for leaving it there, demonstrating (to
the Attwater boys or whoever has followed in their
wake as scourges of Main Street property) that he isn't
intimidated by the word FUCK. In fact, I suspect that
Henry finds it also gives him the chance to suggest to
people that it isn't really an old Anglo-Saxon word but is
derived from the initialed abbreviation of the phrase For
Unlawful Carnal Knowledge, once found in magistrate's
reports.

Next door to Henry's is the old Baptist church. It has
been converted by a lady with Oriental tastes, in high
style and at low cost. Now with willows, Indonesian
flowerpots, a fence craftily constructed of old white
shutters, and Victorian stained-glass windows, the former
church presents an exotic touch that is less incongruous
on the Main Street of a New England seafaring town
than many traditionally minded newer residents might
think. Stonington ships used to sail to Macao and Canton.
A retired seafaring man, the President of the Historical
Society, and his wife are to be seen at dinner as I pass
their house a few doors on. It once belonged to Captain
Fanning, who sailed the *Betsy*, first American ship to
circumnavigate the world. The curtains are drawn back
so that anyone going by may see how an Early American couple ate. The antique furniture is impressive. The

candlelight is atmospheric (though perhaps to be really in keeping with a time when candles were very expensive, oil lamps might be more correct). A few years ago the clapboard front of the house was entirely renewed with new clapboarding cut and routed in late eighteenth-century style, and painted in the appropriate creamy brown Valley Forge mud color. From here it is only a few yards to the Portuguese Holy Ghost Club. The Portuguese began to arrive in the 1840's, at first picked up in the Azores and the Cape Verdes by whaling ships in need of crew. Now, somewhat disguised under names like Henry and Roderick, they form nearly half the population of the village.

Approaching Cannon Square, I make out the bulky shape of Miss Trumbull, dressed in the old sweater and trousers she wears year-round, sitting in the dark on her collapsing, unpainted, vine-covered porch. I hear her say to her old golden cocker spaniel: "Be still. Be still." And then simultaneously we say to each other: "Good evening." Miss Trumbull is one of a long line of Trumbulls who have been pillars of this community, and her house is hungered after by many people. Quite a few are affronted by the fact that it has gone unpainted for at least thirty years, the shutters are disintegrating and the roof shingles rotting, the attic skylight has no glass in it, and the garden is overgrown. At night, no lights appear behind the shabby half-pulled-down brown blinds. For several years Miss Trumbull drove a green Volkswagen which had lost its back window in a parking lot accident at the velvet-mill, where she works; she never replaced the window, but finally traded in the car for a new one. Miss Trumbull is always affable when encountered in Camacho's delicatessen. She has neighbors who polish the copper pipes in their basements. Tonight our "good evenings" ricochet off each other, and I feel distinctly and gratefully that we are two individuals—two human beings aware of one another.

At Cannon Square, which is smaller than Wadawanuck Square, Water and Main Streets again come together. In front of the Greek Revival columns of the village bank (a branch of the Hartford National Bank and Trust Company), two black cannon point to the south and southwest—iron barrels on wheeled wooden carriages. In August, 1814, from a site near the present Plax office building, these guns fired at a small fleet of British ships attacking the town. In a big glass case in the bank, over the filing box of savings account records, is displayed the flag flown by the defenders over their battery, and among the sixteen stars and sixteen stripes are the voids—like giant moth holes—made by the British cannonballs. In winter, children, walking home from school, play on the guns, sitting astride the barrels as if on horseback. My daughter Liz once found a silver dollar an arm's length inside one of the barrels. I wonder if the person who put it there knew that a child would find it, and that it was the sort of thing a child would never forget. One cannon points at a corner of the white house on the south side of the square. This was formerly Captain Thomas Swan's tavern, where the defenders of 1814 regaled each other with tales of their heroism. The other cannon points at Plax.

Now and then we hear rumors that Plax, which makes plastic bottles, is about to close, and there are residents—particularly on Main Street, where the heavily loaded trucks rumble—who wouldn't be unhappy if it did. The long, three-story brick building looms over a section of Water Street, keeping out the sun. Every evening at six the factory chimney lets out a blast of black, acrid smoke, and the change of every shift creates traffic. Real-estate agents think of how many prime waterfront house sites they could conjure out of the property. Nautically inclined conservationists speculate about marine laboratories or oyster hatcheries to make fit use of the spot. On the other hand, I (liking it the way it is) tend to make malicious suggestions that the place (which is usually called "the shop," short for workshop) would make a splendid giant discount store, converted like many other former New England mills, with its present discreetly lighted Monsanto company sign replaced by garish advertisements heralding the day's or week's specials. The Big M. It has had plenty of prior uses. In the oldest part, a handsome masonry building overlooking the harbor, once operated the Trumbull Horseshoe Nail Company. The Joslyn Firearms Company took over in 1861, but went out of business with the end of the Civil War. In 1866 the Standard Braid Company was a brief tenant, after which the Atwoods established their manufactory of machines for the making of silk goods. In its heyday Atwood's produced 80 per cent of the world's silk-manufacturing machinery. When Atwood's shut up shop in 1945 there was a dubious period in which it seemed as if the factory was closed forever; but Clarence Wimpfheimer, who ran the velvet mill, talked the Plax company into taking over. Now, in the plastic age, the factory works three shifts. On the lower-than-street-level ground floor the men at their lathes look out at the legs of young mothers, walking their children to the beach. At night, as I stroll by, I look in to see a machinist with a micrometer measuring the aluminum mold he is making. You can hear hammering, tapping, and drilling, and all sorts of machine hums and whines. During their lunch break the men sit on the low retaining wall running around Cannon Square and discuss baseball and cars and the cost of going to a doctor. The factory is a good prevention of quaintness; it removes from the village a possibly "cute" edge.

At the Point, above a stone commemorating the 1814 battle, looms a grandiloquent flagpole, topped by a golden eagle weathervane which generally seems a little out of phase with the flag below. The pole was a notion of the village Chamber of Commerce. A collection box has been installed at the base to help pay for it and for the flags—a small fifty-star model, flown in windy

weather, and a larger flag reserved for nice days and special occasions—one assumes it was a giant, economy-size
bargain, because it has only forty-eight stars. A constant
slap and ting of halliards comes from the aluminum pole.
Round-about one hears music from car radios, accompanied at night by a nearly silent throb from entwined and
huddled teenage forms. Far enough away from the one
street light overlooking the beach, the darkness is firm.
Stars flicker. On the outer breakwater flashes a white
beacon, and from the inner breakwater another that is
green.

I amble back up the beginning slope of Water Street
and turn right on Omega. Omega is the last cross street
in town. The name makes one wonder whether they
were all classicists in the mid-nineteenth century, putting
columns on their houses and names like Troy and Ithaca
on their towns, or wonder if it were just the jargon of
the time, like Blast off and A-OK. I imagine a contemporary model city called Scenesville, with better-class
housing on Uptight Avenue. Here, halfway up Omega,
lives Joe Mello: trim little house, trim garden, and a trim
garden shed which in the mid-1920's used to be packed
to the roof with gin, Scotch, rye, and rum, landed by
night at Joe Osling's dock by the corner of Omega and
Hancox Street. Osling's dock went in the 1938 hurricane.

It is seventy-five yards along School Street, on the
top of the hill, to my house. On someone's roof an antenna motor whirrs and the antenna turns, changing
channels. But most of the lights are out in the other

houses, where the men rise at six for the morning shift at Electric Boat, in Groton. On Main Street, summer people often leave on a light when they are back in the city, to keep burglars out; in fact, the inhabited houses are those that are blacked out at ten, as the occasionally delinquent boys—the local petty thieves—probably know. People get up early here. When we first lived in Henry Chapin's house we were disappointed that it took Herbert O'Keefe, the plumber, two days to come round to fix a leak. But when he showed up at lunchtime he said that he had been round the last two mornings at seven-thirty, and not getting any response, assumed we were away. On School Street as I walk along I look at the parked cars and see whether mine is boxed in or is boxing anyone else's in. Here many of the houses are two-family, without garages, and many families have teenage children with cars. In several cases the territorial imperative manifests itself in individuals thinking they own the patch of road in front of their houses, and sometimes that in front of other people's houses too.

I step up onto my porch. A cool gust of wind wafts down the street, and as I go in I whistle two notes to let Margot, my wife, know I'm back—it's me. I shut the door behind me and turn the lock. When we go out or away we leave the house unlocked; but at night, at home, perhaps from a feeling of being defenseless while asleep, we bolt the doors, rolling the stone into the mouth of the cave.

⤐ 2 ⤗

SUMMER IS GENERALLY ANNOUNCED on School Street
with a fight. The windows are open, the screens are in,
and on Sunday morning I can hear the Pasquales, just
home from Mass, going at it. Mr. P, having parked his
gleaming washed-twice-a-week Pontiac, yells at Mrs. P,
"Don't be so dumb! She ain't going anyplace today!"
His stentorian high-pitched voice is not much different
from Mrs. Pasquale's as she yells back from the kitchen,
over the noise of her washing machine, "I didn't say she
was going, so who's dumb!" Other doors and windows
open, and several women come out to sweep their steps
and see if this is going to develop into the real thing.
Mrs. Lambrecht's upstairs window goes up with an aluminum clatter and then a mop comes out and shakes vio-
lently for a moment; next a pillow, followed by some
blankets that are left over the windowsill. Mrs.
Lambrecht has retained not only a Cockney accent but
her British prejudices about airing bedclothes; but she is
not just listening to the Pasquales. She is doing what she
would be doing anyway.

With open windows I hear Mrs. Vevarous coming

(17)

home from her day with the Trowbridges, who have
bought the Stickney mansion on Wamphassuc Point, on
the far side of the harbor, and—according to a lady of
artistic taste—"super-Sloaned it." Mrs. Vevarous once
worked for the Trowbridges when they were summer
people, and now once a week Mr. Trowbridge comes in
one of his cars to pick her up, halting with engine running outside her door. I hear his "Good morning, Mary"
and the gray-haired old lady reply, "Good morning, Mr.
Trowbridge." I gather her day with them is now more
of a social than a working occasion. On weekday mornings Mr. Narcizzi walks up the street just after eight
from the night shift at Plax, newspaper and lunch box
under one arm. Mrs. Neto at nine comes out to call
something over to Mrs. Lambrecht. The women of the
street have indoor and outdoor voices—the outdoor voice
honeyed, smiling, rather put-on; the indoor voice loud,
growling, good for screaming at children and sometimes,
outdoors, for yelling at Henry Wilson about the way he
parks his car. At nine thirty Mrs. Evelyn Cole, the
seventy-nine-year-old real estate lady, honks the horn of
her Studebaker outside the Narcizzis', and Mrs. Narcizzi
comes out to collect Mrs. Cole's weekly basket of laundry from the back seat. I suppose the day will come when
all the women on School Street have washers *and* driers
—at the moment, respecting their electricity bills, most
of them do without the latter. By lunchtime on washdays
they are out in their yards or, if they are tenants of an

upstairs apartment, have opened and are leaning out of a second-floor window to peg their wash to clotheslines that run through squeaky galvanized pulleys. While they do this they call over to neighbors who are doing the same next door. The two-family houses have two-family clotheslines running to the backs of the houses from a high Cross of Lorraine at the foot of each garden. The women get a great deal of pleasure from seeing their wash well hung out, the white sheets draped in symmetrical arcs between the clothes pegs, men's shirts nipped neatly by the tail, and socks all hanging with their toes pointing in the same direction.

In turn, what is known about us is certainly greater than the knowledge neighbors would have of us in the city. Drawn curtains proclaim our late rising habits, just as electric lights turned on and garbage cans put out the night before for early morning pick-up let people know we go to bed pretty late. We have more security than privacy. Not many cars pass down the street, and any car stopping attracts the attention of several householders. From my attic study I can see who is calling on the Arrudas or on Mrs. Neto—once a week in the afternoon an insurance man calls to collect Mrs. Neto's weekly premium. She doesn't like to pay it. The insurance man knocks on the door—he knocks and knocks—Mrs. Neto doesn't answer. After a while he starts calling, in soothing tones, "Mrs. Ne-to, Mrs. Ne-to." When this doesn't produce the desired effect, he walks down the street to a few other houses to collect from other clients, perhaps checks to make sure that Mrs. Neto's florid pink Oldsmobile is parked in the neighborhood (so he knows she really is at home), and finally goes back to her door again, knocking more loudly now, and shouting, "Come on, Teresa, open up. I know you're in there." This works. Mrs. Neto appears, in a vivid dressing gown, the door is opened wide enough to let the insurance man in, and in a minute or so he reappears, the account book in his hand having one more figure in it.

One day a young man named Curt Lynch brought back some sailing gear I'd lent him. Curt was home for a week before going overseas for Army Intelligence. He had parked with two wheels on the opposite sidewalk, and then come over and stood talking at my front door. Suddenly he half-turned; his eyes lit up—they don't seem to be able to train you so that you can stop your eyes lighting up. "Golly," he said, "do you know there are at least four people standing behind different windows of the house across the street, watching us?" Curt was brought up out in the country.

If there is anything like a fight in the street, for instance, between the Morrises and Henry Wilson about the Morrises' rose bush, which Wilson chopped down because it was touching his fence, or between Mrs. Dollart and Mrs. Neto, because the young Dollart boys have been calling Billy Neto a sissy, or because Mrs. Neto, tired of hearing Mrs. Dollart refer to the holy candles

burning in her front window on a feast day as black su-
perstition, has called Mrs. Dollart (to her face) a heathen
devil (and Mrs. Dollart well known to put aside her
Protestant ethic to attend the Tuesday night Bingo at
St. Mary's Catholic basement)—then, when the combat-
ants are out in the street, people do more than peek
around curtains or lift the venetian blinds. They start
polishing their front doorknobs and washing their cars,
anything to get a better view. Mrs. Cabral has a finely
tuned sense of knowing who is on the street, and will
pop out of her front door, as if she were going somewhere, looking surprised to see me climbing on my bicy-
cle to get the morning paper, and then, depending on
whether she is currently a saleswoman for the *World
Book,* Avon Cosmetics, or local real estate, will say,
"Oh, good morning, say, does your wife use Gardenia
Cream lipstick?" or "I was wondering if you have any
friends who might be interested in this little property
I've just got listed—only in the low twenties—a good
buy."

We went away one weekend and let some friends use
the house. On Monday morning, as I bought the *Times*
from him, Frankie Keane said, "I saw lights on in your
house Saturday night. Since you were away, I thought I
ought to tell you." I've developed similar traits, glancing
out of the front-room window to see if the car then
being parked has locked bumpers with mine, and keeping
an eye on the garbage cans of my next-door neighbors,

the Tripps. Sometimes I put them out if they forget to, or put them back in if they forget that. On rainy evenings, I occasionally sneak into their yard to move the can which sits under a leaky gutter of ours, and otherwise pings loudly all night.

I'm not sure whether this Stonington system would prevent an unpremeditated murder, but it would probably turn up ample evidence about the criminal—and that may well furnish a deterrent to premeditated crime. I read recently in a study of the formation of American small towns (*As a City Upon a Hill*, by Professor Page Smith) that when Longmont, Colorado, was established in the late 1860's, its founders declared in their charter: "No man is integral within himself. We are all parts of one grand community, and it behooves every man to know what his neighbor is about."

❧ 3 ❧

OUR HOUSES ARE WOODEN. Being made of wood, they are malleable. My house was built in the 1860's of simple balloon construction, which was made possible by the invention of machine-made nails, and did away with the old slow framing methods using posts, girts, beams, and braces. Studs and interior frames were quickly put up, floor beams thrown across from wall to wall, a roof stuck on above, and then the exterior clapboarding nailed on to hold it all together—it used to be called "Chicago construction." When I first saw my house it was a miserable February day, a good day for house-hunting, since presumably a house then looked as bad as it ever could. Once 16 School Street had been painted yellow. On this particular day it had—where paint remained—rather the color of dirty sand. In most places the grain of the wood showed like salt- and wind-weathered skin. Under a not quite congruous porch large patches of brick were exposed where the stucco had peeled from the foundation. The porch struck an artificial note on what was essentially a plain façade: from the top down, an attic window under the inverted

V of the roof, three second-floor windows (each with twelve panes of glass), and then two downstairs windows set to the right of the front door with an ugly square window occupying its upper half. The door, moreover, was covered by a flimsy aluminum storm door with ornate aluminum grillwork surrounding a letter "R." The Rebellos owned the house. As I stood across the street with the agent and thought how it wasn't at all what we were looking for, I was wondering if the "R" came unscrewed (or did one have to throw the whole door away?), and that the first thing I would do would be to pull off the porch. But the porch, littered with bicycles, doll carriages, and oars, is still there.

Changes have been greater within. Armed with a shovel, hammer, wrecking bar, and iron jemmy, I went to work on the interior partitions. Layers of old newspaper sustained dry horsehair plaster that crumbled readily from laths, themselves nailed to a core of haphazardly matched upright chestnut boards. The shovel was useful for scraping off the plaster. Then each lath had to be loosened at one end with the wrecking bar and pulled away, singly or in batches of three or four. As I did this, rips would appear in the various historic layers of wallpaper, the top rip not always matching the rips in lower strata—the effect was that of a relief map, with contours of different colors. Sometimes small sections of plaster and lath came off, but I felt most successful when a large piece of wall came loose at once, swinging for a moment by a last nail or tenacious thickness of old wallpaper, then crashing to the floor. Plaster dust rose in thick, throat-constricting clouds.

Once you've got over the guilt of destruction, knocking down walls is just hard work. In this case, the guilt disappeared quickly. I was getting rid of wallpaper and walls I didn't like. I was removing the stamp of the previous owners. I was making the house mine. I found thick gloves and thick-soled boots made a difference, for the laths fell half-hidden in plaster, and nails stuck up as often as down, piercing sneakers and old shoes. What surprised me was how much material went into a wall. Stacked up neatly and doing its job, a wall didn't look like much. But demolished, on the floor, it became huge mounds of rubble, out of which lath and board poked forth, awkwardly impeding. After a night or two of trying to work over and around these middens I needed help.

The man to get was Bill D'Amico. People said this who had direct experience of house reconstruction or the imaginative ability to put themselves in my dusty boots. Others gave names of contractors who were both hard to get and expensive to pay. Bill, on the other hand, was the garbage collector. He had a Popeye-like figure of which he was clearly proud—arms whose bulging muscles he exposed with neatly rolled-up sleeves, and a tight belted waist under a powerful chest. He was alleged to be an accomplished electric guitar player and was certainly an ingenious mechanic whose collection of old vehicles around his patchwork-fronted house in the low ground behind the Borough School gave birth or helping parts to other vehicles: dune buggies, snow ploughs, and the army surplus garbage truck.

These days the village garbage is picked up by an efficient Mystic firm, with a fully mechanized sanitation vehicle and three or four cheerful and industrious men. They move swiftly through the streets of the village on Tuesday and Friday mornings. The garbage cans are where one has left them on the sidewalk, the lids on, and empty. In Bill's time it was different. Bill's truck had sides fenced with old doors, and a back railed with cardboard boxes collected en route. His helper-henchman was a young, black-haired, similarly muscled man with cold eyes that gave the whole endeavor an air of menace. But this feeling may have been merely a householder's reaction to the fact that you knew that if Bill and his colleague didn't feel like picking up your garbage, they wouldn't. They were down on people who tried to stomp too much into a single garbage can, making the can excessively heavy and reluctant to disgorge its contents when turned upside down. Their physiques were a result of lifting these cans six feet over the palisade of doors. They seemed to be natural men, outcast, doing a job that few other men would want to do. This gave them an edge. If you wanted your garbage cans emptied —and for some reason the idea of not having them emp-

tied built up fantasies of overflowing fly-attracting matter, perhaps springing from an inherited fear of putrefac-
tion and the plague—you had to allow them liberties,
such as parking athwart the street blocking all traffic
while they had a chat with Mrs. Neto, or sticking the
truck's nose into the Previtys' driveway while Bill's
helper went off to get a new battery. If this failed to
start the truck—and by then they were at the foot of
School Street hill, unable to roll the truck and get it
going—it might sit there for a day, attracting seagulls.

Bill cleared out my downstairs rubble in quick time.
The word went rapidly down School Street, parked cars
were wisely moved away, and Bill backed his truck up
over the curb and against the porch. The lower half of
the front-room windows were propped open. Out went
boards, lath, and plaster in broad shovelsful. When it was
all gone, two truck loads, and the white powdery dust
had settled again, there was room to stand and brood
about what I was going to build in its place. Soon
enough, wood, nails, and plasterboard were coming in. I
had hoped that Bill would help me here, but his truck
finally expired and the title of refuse collector was no
longer attractive; he went to work full time, like so
many local craftsmen, at Electric Boat, the nuclear
submarine builders in Groton. I found the son of a house
wrecker—the son preferring building to wrecking—
who assisted me in putting up the main beam in the living room—a fir ten by four, twenty-two feet long. I

became a frequent visitor at the Stonington lumberyard, and when the money to pay my carpenter ran out, became an energetic rough-and-ready carpenter myself.

Wood is a material that can be shaped, which takes the stamp of the person shaping it; thus carpentry is an expression of character. My neighbor Peter Tripp talks of a man out west—known as Nevada Joe or some such name—who felt he would die if he stopped building; he had a house to which he added one new room every year. Some of these rooms had mansard roofs, some gabled, some flat-topped, all tacked onto one another. Peter himself goes in for carpentry with great flourishes of improvement. He expresses his need for immortality or simple shelter in louvered porches, gingerbread garden sheds, and ornate garbage-can shelters. He is one moment passionate about the protective qualities of aluminum paint; in the next (the aluminum having proved an unreliable base for the following coat of red that Mary, Peter's wife, has insisted on), he has all the painted clapboards taken off and cedar shingles nailed on. If you look closely at something Peter himself has built, like the garden shed, you see that piece after piece is added, that he has hardly been able to stop adding and embellishing—until his enthusiasm suddenly runs out, and he stops with a jolt altogether. My own carpentry is minimal. I use nails, say, on the backing pieces of cupboard doors, where I should use screws. Joints are visible, undisguised by molding. Nothing ever quite gets properly finished, or to be exactly what I would like it to be. Dissatisfaction is a constant in carpentry as in art. Paul Moody at the lumberyard said to me in those first weeks: "Ah, so you've bought a house—well, you'll never be finished with it." And indeed, some years after that period devoted to tearing up linoleum, hammering studs into place, nailing panels of wallboard over old doorways, and sanding, varnishing, and painting, there are days when the house definitely seems to be falling apart: the stairs collapsing sideways, the downstairs hall floor in need of a lolly column in the cellar to hold it up, one wall (upstairs between a child's bedroom and the bathroom) down at one end by three-quarters of an inch so that there is a gap between it and the ceiling, while the joint where it meets the outside wall looks like a diagram of a rift valley or the San Andreas Fault. There are water stains—from bathtub overflow—on the living-room ceiling that require at least four coats of paint to cover them. Doors swing poorly on their hinges; some don't close at all; others, on cupboards, I build to hide the accumulated chaos on the shelves behind. I have a nightmare infrequently but often enough in which the entire clapboard siding on the north side of the house falls off into Peter's lettuce garden. Why, I sometimes ask myself, do I tinker and fiddle with this ridiculous house, painting and sawing, when I could spend the same time making money and pay carpenters and painters to do the job half-decently? The only answer must be: It is

my nature. This house is me, unfinished, slightly dilapi-
dated, with one large and somewhat charming room, and
different centers of focus, nothing hard and concentrated
—a magpie house reflecting its owner's magpie mind,
full of nice places, interesting corners, untidy spots and
dull, banal, or untended stretches: a house that is good in
bright sunlight or warm firelight, and not much between.

But I have found something here I enjoy, even as I
moan at having to do it. This is spackling; the word itself
gives me pleasure. Spackling is a rite, a guild mystery.
Walls I rebuilt with panels of plasterboard, and the joints
between had to be covered with paper tape, laid in, and
afterwards covered with spackle, a thin, gluey plaster. It
was a skill to be mastered. The thin plaster cement had
to be the correct consistency, neither too much nor too
little water, and no lumps. While I was laying the first
coat of this along and in the crack between the gypsum
panels, a suitable seven- or eight-foot length of paper tape
sat soaking in a pan of water. I ran this through my fin-
gers, mangle-fashion, to remove excess water. Then I laid
it on the joint, running the trowel down from the top to
get rid of wrinkles. Over this, after it was somewhat
dried, went a second layer of spackle, and this was where
the art seemed to come in—although as in art much de-
pended on the substance and stability of one's ground-
work. I realized this after a while, that it was harder to
achieve a smooth, barely perceptible joint with the

covering layer of plaster if the lower layer weren't of the right width or thickness, and if the tape weren't properly moistened and unwrinkled. With the top layer, the broader it was the more difficult to achieve an absolutely smooth surface, but the less chance of the tape showing through at the edges when the plaster dried. To get smoothness, the trick was to have a perfectly clean trowel, as broad in blade as one could handle, dipped in clean water, and to hold it at just the right angle of incidence as—with just the right amount of pressure—one drew the trowel over the seam. It is the kind of job which requires the proper touch. Some days one has it. It seems to depend on one's digestion, mood, and the atmospheric pressure. You can make out most of the joints I spackled then.

4

AT NIGHT I sometimes leave the sidewalks and walk in the road. The streets are empty then, except for a perambulating cat or stray dog and occasionally—perhaps in Water Street near Roland's Market—a small, black-and-white shape which scuttles across the road, nose down, tail high. We used to have a baby-sitter named Mary Madeira, who wouldn't walk the hundred yards to her home unaccompanied. This wasn't because she was afraid of murderers or molesters, but because she was scared to death of skunks. The lady who formerly ran an antique shop next to the Higleys once told them, in neighborly fashion, that a skunk lived under their house. She'd seen it coming and going. Carol Higley, desperate, called us for good advice, but all I could suggest was that she ask the watchful antique woman to tell her when the skunk had gone out for a stroll and then rush around and block up the opening it used. This didn't appeal to Carol. She said, "What if it has left all its babies behind?"

This may have been the same skunk, or family of skunks, that lived under the Lewises' house. However, when friends later discussed buying the house from them, Daphne Lewis called it a woodchuck—she claimed, moreover, that her husband Yale had got rid of them. Yale was communications officer on a submarine. Home on leave between patrols, he found he was unable to sleep—the silence of the village nights was enlivened by gnawing sounds from beneath the polished oak bedroom floor. Since he wanted to preserve the floor and his health, and didn't want to use traps or poison gas, Yale attempted to expel the animals by peaceful means. One night when the noise began, Yale retaliated by knocking on the floor just above what he took to be the so-called woodchucks' nest. Then, slowly tapping, he proceeded along a line between the nest and the hole they used in the foundations. His idea was that the woodchucks would move ahead of the threatening sound from above. When Yale reached the interior wall, which was as far as he could go, he got up and dashed outside, quickly blocking the opening with a stone. I don't believe anyone checked with Yale to discover whether or not he'd heard the alleged woodchucks again. An English newspaperman lived in the house for a while a year later, and back in England wrote a story about his stay in America, making much of the prevalence of wildlife in settled communities, and winding up with an account of the skunks that had lived under his house in Stonington.

Farm animals are supposed to be prohibited by village ordinance, though Eleanor Perenyi says she's often been waked at dawn by a cockerel crowing on Grand Street. Dogs abound in the village, and cats thrive, especially those who live in a partly wild state on the town dock, where the fish is landed. In this particular feline epoch a breed of extra-toed orange cats flourishes—cats skilled at insinuating themselves into the households of summer tenants or new winter residents. A few mangy old-timers prowl daily through our garden on a traditional shortcut between Hancox and Water Street. Formerly they used the garden of my neighbor, Peter Tripp, as well, but Peter has arranged all sorts of obstacles for them, nailing chicken wire in the corners of fences, and running an almost invisible strand of monofilament fishing line along the tops of the fence pickets. Cats, jumping into his yard, are neatly booby-trapped.

Many of the village dogs serve little purpose other than to scratch the dirt and yap in the yards in which they are kept shut up—erstwhile watchdogs and survivors of the infrequent raids made by Mr. Davis, the dog warden. Mr. Davis farms on the Pawcatuck River. Farming seems to take most of his time and energy, and in his subsidiary career as town dog-catcher he reacts only to an accumulation of complaints in the local press about his diligence and ability, and angry telephone calls made directly to the Borough Warden or the Town First Selectman. When—perhaps because a child has been bitten or garbage cans have been turned over—the public need has been sufficiently proclaimed, Mr. Davis makes a foray into the village. His blue pick-up truck is sometimes spotted as it comes over the viaduct. Children then run ahead of it through the streets, yelling, "The dog-catcher's in town—he's caught Dusty!" "Mrs. Dodson's trying to find Rabbit before Mr. Davis gets him." This alarm system helps, but it doesn't prevent Mr. Davis from making some notable captures. On one raid he took in the poodle of Father Loftus, the parish priest. Several eminent parishioners tried to lean on Mr. Davis, but he wouldn't budge. He said, "He'll have to pay the fine like anyone else. I don't care if it's the Pope's dog."

Rabbit is one of the half-dozen dogs of real character in the place—an easy mark. He is a Chesapeake Bay retriever, with a light cocoa-brown velvety coat, gray nose, and reddish eyes—the latter feature being why Johnny Dodson, his former owner, called him Rabbit. It was also Johnny's idea that Rabbit would be a splendid duck dog, one of those creatures who function as the long arm of the hunter, bringing back downed birds from remote fastnesses in marsh and swamp. Rabbit, however, had no disposition for this; he preferred running up and down in front of the duck blind, letting the ducks know what was going on. During one expedition I made with Johnny to Sandy Point, the island to the east of the village in Little Narragansett Bay, I kept Rabbit amused inside the duck blind while Johnny stalked down the beach for a few successful shots. On trips we made to Wamphassuc Point, supposedly for pheasant but more profitable in tomatoes and grapes, poached from the Stickney gardens, Rabbit rollicked through the undergrowth, chasing chipmunks. Most summers Rabbit stayed with a trainer on Fishers Island, and came home on Labor Day looking sleek. During the other seasons he lived in a pen at the boatyard. He sometimes howled all night for Johnny—the noise infuriated the neighbors. He often went for long walks with strangers, and if children threw sticks for him he would plunge into the harbor in the iciest weather. Occasionally Rabbit escaped from his pen and hotfooted to the school, where he bounded into second-grade enrichment periods or joined in basketball practice. Mr. La Chance, who was the principal, would then phone Johnny at the boatyard: "Your dog's at the school. The children are chasing him round the corridors." And on a rising note of desperation: "Please come at once."

In late winter when the woods are bare, deer now and then run among the houses. A doe a few years ago swam across the nearly frozen harbor and, perhaps blind with hunger, seeing the distance rather than the foreground, plunged through the picture window of a cottage on Northwest Street. It rampaged around the kitchen in fright while the equally frightened lady of the house telephoned for help. Then, pursued by the Pioneer Fire Engine and crew, it jumped out through the window again and dashed off across the old railroad yard.

In a humid spring or summer there are problems

with wildlife on a miniature, more personal scale. Proximity in school classrooms and borrowed hairbrushes are blamed for the spread of headlice, and suddenly all the children seem to have close-cropped hair. A flea-collar unthinkingly strapped on a cat causes a flea to jump (by its fantastic, disproportionately powerful jumping mechanism) onto us. Ticks are brought back from walks on Wamphassuc or Napatree. But in all seasons the pre-eminent wildlife of the village consists of gulls, denizens of Sandy Point. The gulls roost in the declivities and pockets of the island's central ridge. Some stand guard in front of their nests, heads poking above the marram grass, and later walk their young down to the water or fly above them, diving and shrieking at intruders. They are big birds, and there seems to be more and more of them. In spring the ex-officio officials of the beach association used to burn the grass on Sandy Point in an attempt to destroy some of the nests—and perhaps thereby contributed to the instability of the island and encouraged its slow movement across Little Narragansett Bay toward the village. The gulls are there every summer in greater quantities. They are said to be driving out the terns, with which they formerly coexisted. They are great scavengers; the town dump feeds them, and they prey on baby horseshoe crabs, creatures which have managed to survive more or less unchanged for several hundred million years but may find themselves tipped into oblivion in the next half century, the way we're going. In winter the gulls perch on the village rooftops, sometimes sitting on chimneys as they warm their feathers over the hot exhaust from furnaces, or, suddenly spotting an edible item, swooping down into a back yard, sending the sparrows and starlings flying off in a nervous twitter. In late afternoons the gulls hang in the wind over Stonington Point, watching the tide eddies and the churned-up wakes of incoming fishing draggers, making sounds, *scrah, scrah,* as they wheel and dive. An exception to these thriving winter gulls was one I came across last January, running haphazardly along Water Street. It was a young gull. It looked like a big, brown, feathery egg to which head, legs, and feet had been attached—no wings were visible; perhaps it couldn't fly. I was driving the car, but as I slowed down the gull darted aside into a yard like a tiny ostrich with bolas-twirling gauchos after it.

On Sandy Point two Januarys ago I saw a Great Snowy Owl. To me, the sandy island is an extension of the village, and I try to get out to it every month of the year, sometimes to walk, sometimes to sit, and sometimes as on this occasion to land only for a moment before re-embarking. The owl had built his solitary nest on a mound at the southernmost end of the island, where he had water a few yards away on both sides. At first, as I rowed by, I thought he was stuffed, a decoy like those used on motorboats to keep the gulls, and gulls' droppings, off the decks (on sailing boats, masts and rigging seem to serve that purpose). The owl sat, very upright and very still. I had to get close to the beach in order to see his eyes move—they seemed to revolve around his head in a fixed plane. This illusion was the result of an overall camouflage effect of white feathers and brown markings, and I had landed before I saw that his head in fact moved as well as those eyes kept haughtily trained upon me. I walked toward him. I hoped that he would take off so that I could see him flying. I shouted, "Hey, owl!" but he didn't budge. It was I who had to leave. Apparently when the lemmings are in short supply in the Arctic these great owls come south. Roger Tory Peterson writes in one of his guidebooks that their visits are cyclic, once every four years. Peterson also calls the bird simply the Snowy Owl, though he is generally larger than the Great Horned Owl, and from what I saw of him equally warrants that extra "Great."

❦ 5 ❧

OUR OWN MIGRATIONS FOR FOOD—the supply being plentiful—are affected by cost. Roland's, the Stonington Market, and Camacho's, the three village food stores, in general charge more for their goods than do the larger chain stores in Mystic and Westerly. It isn't long, some twenty years or so, since there was a store on nearly every street in the village; for sugar or salt or a box of matches you had only to go down the street or around the corner. The little buildings are still there, some used as garages or ground-floor attics, some converted into living quarters with curtains hung gipsy-tea-parlor style across the plate-glass windows. The store on School Street now belongs to a navy couple, who rent it out when they are away to people who seem to suit the still half-converted nature of the place: poor families with many children, pale with late-night television and a diet of potato chips and soda pop; or groups of young submariners with big cars and expensive motorcycles—when they finally leave we realize again that we live on one of the quietest streets in a small town anywhere in the industrial world. Mrs. Sadie Cunha, a seventy-four-

year-old lady who now and then babysits for us, was
telling me the other night what she and her husband
lived on when they were first married in 1914. He
brought home eighteen dollars a week after—in her
words—he got his trade as a machinist (he worked in the
Atwood shop, now Plax); and of those eighteen, five
were immediately put in a building loan association. Their
rent, for a ground-floor apartment in a house on Trumbull Street, was two dollars a week. On groceries and
kerosene for cooking she spent two dollars and sixty
cents a week. "Things were cheaper then," said Mrs.
Cunha, meaning relatively cheaper. "You were putting
something by, you could save something." Mr. Cunha
also got two dollars and fifty cents a month from Mrs.
Stanton, at whose house he fixed the furnace, raked
ashes, put out the rubbish, and did the garden. He always
had a boat, and Mrs. Cunha says he used to put a new engine in it every few years. She still lives in the small
house on Omega Street they moved to from the Trumbull Street apartment, a block away. She is proud of the
fact that she has lived in only two places since the day
she married.

We spend thirty-five dollars or so a week at the
A & P in Westerly, and probably another ten or fifteen
in the village stores—a total sum that a recent *New York
Times* calls the bare minimum for a family of four (and
we are six) to spend on groceries in the New York metropolitan area. We are outside that area, which helps; but

we are probably encouraging the creation of our own smaller metropolitan area by not shopping for everything in the village and by often driving instead to a larger place to buy more cheaply in quantity. The people who seem to do all their shopping in the village are the rich and the hard-up. The Netos down the street have their groceries delivered by Roland's truck. At Stonington Market, where we indulge ourselves by buying the good vegetables and, now and then, feeling well off, the good meat, wealthier folk send or phone in their shopping lists and pay their bills monthly.

Sometimes I find in a coat pocket or the glove compartment of the car a list in my wife's neat writing, made on the back of a mimeographed note from the school or a cardboard lid from a children's game from which some of the indispensable parts have been lost. The list is for food already long ago consumed: cans of Italian tomatoes, tomato paste, a package of Italian hot sausages, two cans of orange juice, English muffins, Wheat Chex. And though the meals themselves are past—the conversations and indigestion that went with them not even a memory —I find that reading a statement of what we lived on has an interest, perhaps an archeological, time-capsule sort of interest. Hamburger and chicken pot pies (five for eighty-nine cents), a piece of ham and a package of Lamb Combination, cod, haddock, or (maybe) bluefish, rice, noodles, spaghetti number eight (four packages), lasagna, Rice Krispies, two frozen vegetables, three fresh vege-

tables, lettuce, tomatoes, oranges, apples, bananas, mushrooms, carrots, onions, sometimes cherries, peaches, and
grapefruit, marmalade, peanut butter, jelly, ketchup, soda,
tonic water, flat bread (which is what the children call
the rubbery stuff they prefer), butter, margarine, cheese,
and sandwich meat. And of course we also need floor
wax, Ivory Snow, tooth paste, soap, shampoo, toilet
paper, paper towels, and (in season) Kleenex, Vicks, and
aspirin. I have forgotten eggs. The variety of this list is
staggering if you jump back only a little more than a
hundred years, when most food was seasonal and, for
most people, consistently monotonous; bread was the
staff of life and the measure of existence.

Although we use the larger-town supermarkets, I
continue to feel guilty about it. What in some ways
makes the village is our ability to walk to a store for ne-
cessities, and if everyone shopped in our middle-income,
cost-conscious way the village markets would not exist.*
There wouldn't perhaps be any great decline in cheerful
shopping—the people who work in the Westerly A & P
are a good deal more sincerely friendly than those who
serve in one of our smaller grocery stores. The village
stores have to pay more for their goods because they buy
in smaller quantity from wholesalers. We have to pay a
little more for convenience, for the opportunity to pop
in, in passing, or to hand a child a couple of dollars and

---

* In recent years the village has lost its shoe repair shop, its jeweler,
and its funeral home.

say, "Run down to Mr. Siegel's and get yourself a new pair of sneakers."

Mr. Siegel is the owner of the Stonington Department Store. He often isn't in the store when a customer enters; he may be across the street at Ed's Cleaning, or up at Squadrito's Barber Shop, returning the barber shop copy of the *Daily News*. Although he isn't there, you can walk around the deserted store (which is actually one large ground-floor room crammed with clothes counters, shelves, and cardboard boxes from which merchandise has not yet been unpacked) and look for what you want. By the time you have found it, or come to the conclusion Mr. Siegel doesn't have it, in he will come. The children call him Mr. Seagull. He is a plump, egg-shaped man, with tousled gray hair, wearing a white no-iron shirt, silk tie, and button-front wool cardigan, who gives you a look of affable inquiry rather than a spoken question as he asks what you want.

In summer I buy a pair of sneakers and a tennis hat from Mr. Siegel. In fall I generally buy a pair of corduroys and some socks. Time was when I got a slight markdown, or at least a remission of state tax, which Mr. Siegel took upon himself, but these days Mr. Siegel no longer seems to think me in danger of abandoning his store for a Giant Drive-In Discount Clothing Center, and I pay full price. (I admit the full price quoted by Mr. Siegel is often encouragingly less than the price marked on the box—"See," he'll say, "I'm charging you

$3.99 and they went up to $4.49 last week.") I pointed out to him that this year's corduroys were two dollars dearer than last year's; up from $5.95 to $7.95. "Two reasons for it!" shouts Mr. Siegel, who is either deaf or finds that a strident fair-ground voice is good for business. "The cost of living! Everything's up! And—second —these are Perma Press—no iron—all baked in ovens!" He adds, in a final rousing cheer: "If you don't like 'em, bring 'em back! You know my policy."

Mr. Siegel has three brothers, also in the haberdashery business in various parts of Connecticut. If you go into his store on a weekday morning for a pair of 9½ sneakers, which he doesn't have in stock, he will say, "Sold the last pair yesterday! But I can get 'em for you by Friday." And so, from one brother or another, the sneakers come—the Siegels having at their mutual disposal a stock of goods effectively three times larger than that in the store each of them possesses.

Clearly, to run a store is to hand over a good part of yourself to the world. Mrs. Hirsch of Camacho's will spend minutes helping a child pick out several cents' worth of candy. Some people get tempted by the idea of being shopkeepers and set themselves up selling antiques, exotic foods, or handcrafted leather goods, and sometimes they succeed, even though the demand hasn't been evident and their stuff is neither good nor cheap, because people realize that running a store isn't going to be just a hobby or a pastime with them—it is entirely what they mean to do. Mr. Camacho is thus someone one may identify pre-eminently as a cutter of sliced salami, a maker of grinders, a man whose watering of window plants and letting down of awnings are the visible mechanics of being a delicatessen proprietor. Camacho's, we call the place, even though the outside sign in large letters says I.G.A. Market. In the village it is hard to think of a successful business that isn't familiarly named—and if not named, called, for one refers to Stonington Market as Wiggie's, and to the Book Mart as Dorothy Brown's.

At close quarters, as we are, we have some of the delicate problems the French face—whether to *tutoyer* or *vousvoyer* someone in business; in our case, whether or not to use first names. The liquor store used to be run by Paul Schepis, an elderly Italian gentleman I always called—because of his age and dignified bearing—Mr. Schepis. When he retired, he handed over the active management to his grandson Charles Chiappone, a large, cordial young man whom the customers all call Charlie. After a few months of doing the same, and having Charlie in reply call me Mr. Bailey, I took the plunge. I was buying our weekly gallon of red Fior di California. I said, "Charlie, why don't you call me Tony?" Charlie smiled, a bit embarrassed. "Oh, I couldn't do that, Mr. Bailey, it wouldn't be right. I wasn't brought up that way." We had a difficult period for the next week or so. I felt as though I had made him feel like an encyclopedia salesman. I couldn't bring out "Mr. Chiappone" and no longer quite felt justified in calling him "Charlie." But it wasn't many bottles of wine and cashed checks later that we were back in an orthodox young businessman-respected customer relationship, with me calling him Charlie and him calling me Mr. Bailey, as if nothing had ever upset this delicate balance. At the gas station, Al Palmer had a few months of calling me Tony—it coincided with my ownership of a declining Renault Dauphine, which spent much of the time at his establishment. Now, with a going Saab, I am back at Mister. Roland, proprietor of one of the local grocery markets, has days when he calls me Tony and other days when he just nods, but with him it may be the effect of the weather or the general state of trade. With Bob Stillman at Bindloss Fuel and Hardware I have arrived at an intermediate stage where to call each other Mister this or that obviously strikes us as too formal, but we haven't yet found the moment to make the leap to first names. Is it the people who have no village competition or simply those of warm and open character with whom there are no doubts and hesitations? Frankie Keane at the news office, Andy Perry at the lumber yard, and John Victoria at the post office—they and I first-name each other unconcernedly, and sometimes perhaps even with a feeling of pleasure that we respond to one another in such a way that it is the right and proper thing to do.

❧ 6 ❧

THE GLOOMIEST PLACE to pass at night is the Harbor View. Rosy-fingered neon illuminates the cheap brick surround of the bar window, and glancing in I see the long bar with perhaps two men sitting at it, a long way apart—the man who designed the long straight bar had no conception of comradely drinking. The Harbor View is the sole survivor of seven bars that used to thrive in the village. They did well with the success of the fishing fleet roughly until the end of World War II. Charlie's burnt out a few years ago, and is now an apartment house. The Sea Village Restaurant, where you could also get a drink, is now a motel. Apart from the Harbor View, the only drinking place is the Portuguese Holy Ghost Club, whose flags (Portuguese and American) fly at half-staff whenever a member dies, and quite a few of its members seem to die every year of drink. When we first came to School Street I used to see one man coming home from the Holy Ghost, moving slowly up the street, stopping now and then to rest against a house, sometimes in midmorning or early afternoon; and then quickly enough he wasn't making it any more—he would be found lying on a sidewalk, or slumped on someone's steps. He went away for a while, presumably to the hospital, and came back looking gray and thin. He sat on his own steps, saying nothing. And then the flags flew at the Holy Ghost.

Most people drink at home. There are two liquor stores, one of which changes hands fairly often, the other, Paul Schepis's, favored by steady custom. At Christmas Mr. Schepis and Charlie Chiappone hand out gifts to their regulars—a bottle of Black Label Johnny Walker, a bottle of champagne—and if you protest, though not too vigorously, Mr. Schepis says "No, no, you're good to me all through the year. At Christmas, I'm good to you." There is generally an official notice posted prominently on the back of the Schepis cash register. It declares that the proprietor, by court order, is not allowed to sell his wares to the person whose name has been typewritten in the blank space provided thereon. Sometimes a woman is named, sometimes a man—there are two "regulars." Alcoholics Anonymous has a substantial membership in the village. One young woman discovered this when, on first moving to the place, she tried to start play readings, and picked Monday night for the inaugural occasion. Only one person showed up, and he explained that she shouldn't be offended; it was simply the night of the AA meeting.

Those who drink moderately and enjoy it, and now and then perhaps get nicely drunk and enjoy it too, may be tempted to say that idleness and overindulgence in liquor go together. Men who "work" at Electric Boat and are underemployed there (as in the case of a member of a welding union waiting several hours for a member of the draftsmen's union to come and chalk a line on which he can weld a fitting)—they drink. Men who sit at home reading the *Wall Street Journal* and brood about the fortune that has made it unnecessary for them ever to have a job—they drink. Yet, even so, we may make more sober use of our greater leisure than our hard-working predecessors did. The Reverend Sherlock Bristol recalled that in the mid-nineteenth century in his home town of Cheshire, Connecticut—a place about the size of Stonington—there were "eight distilleries of cider brandy in full blast, from twenty to thirty cider mills, and half a dozen taverns all selling brandy and whiskey at three cents a glass. . . . Was it strange then that my mother and I counted over fifty drunkards within the circle of our acquaintance? Was it strange that in one winter we buried ten men who died with delirium tremens, out of a population of two thousand people?"

It becomes less surprising that the temperance movement got such a start in New England. On several occasions in the nineteenth century Stonington voted to go dry, and in 1905, when it voted to go wet again, it was only by a majority of five votes. But by the twenties and the time of the Volstead Act, when the whole country went dry, the spirit of Stonington was stronger. You

could walk around the village and hear the tea-kettle
boilers steaming, the sounds of the chaleira in Portuguese
houses going drip, drip, and corks popping. None of the
maintainers of the law much had their hearts in enforc-
ing it. The Coast Guard men when off duty would walk
across to the other side of Bindloss's dock and play poker
with the men off the rum-runners. The local police
didn't consider rum-running to be quite the same as ordinary law-breaking. Joe Mello, who lives on Omega
Street, told me, "There was so much gravy around in
those days the police wanted part of it too. My uncle
used to hand some of it out—he was given money by
two of the big dealers, a Portugee and an Italian guy
who used to stop at the old Rhode Island Hotel in Westerly; they told him to take care of the cops around here.
But there was one cop, Dave Brooker, who figured he
hadn't got his full share. So he pulled a raid on them one
night when they were unloading over on Lord's Point.
My uncle got fined a hundred and a quarter and put inside
for thirty days. Another time the local cops brought in
the state troopers from Groton. They caught my step-
father down at the fishing sheds where Sea Village motel
is now. He knocked out one of the troopers. They shot
at him, and broke one of his legs. Then all the neighbors
came out screaming and there was a little riot and for a
while, till reinforcements came, the troopers stood with
their backs to the sheds. Considering all the guns and
rum and money, there wasn't much bloodshed. Now and

then someone got beaten up. And one night when I was over in Montauk a couple of trucks got hijacked. No one shot to kill."

In Stonington knives flashed now and then when a dealer found a few cases short, and a little pressure was applied until the man who had brought it in from the sea found some that had "accidentally" fallen under the dock during the unloading. There were landing places all around the village. Fishing boats were going in and out all the time as well as the fast boats built for the purpose by one of the shipyards in Mystic—*Black Goose* and *Gander* are two names Joe Mello remembers. One morning a runner named Smiley McCormick dumped his load right in the harbor while being chased by the Coast Guard. People went fishing for bottles for years afterwards. It was, at least in Mr. Mello's memory, a very good time. "I got paid ten cents a case for unloading. The boats averaged five hundred cases aboard, so that made fifty bucks a trip. I was eighteen going on nineteen. It was fun. They'd generally break a case and give each man a bottle. I don't think liquor ever tasted as good afterwards as it did then—at least until they started cutting it right on board the boats with grain alcohol. The first shipments was aged—great stuff."

Walking on summer nights one can drop back into the past on the sounds of lobster boats, the staccato combustion noise from air-cooled exhausts, and the sound of fireworks, the simulation of guns, set off by boys in an-

ticipation of the Fourth. Walking by Cannon Square I
pass the big three-family house built on the site of Captain Thomas Swan's tavern. This was where the stage-
coach used to halt. It was also where a cache of
gunpowder was fortunately discovered during the British attack on the village in August, 1814, when the powder for the defenders' cannon (now in the square opposite the house) had run low. And some nights walking I
remember that I am doing something that one couldn't
always take for granted. In medieval English towns, well
after Magna Carta, one of the precautions taken against
violence and theft was a prohibition of night-walking. In
London in summer one could walk until ten; after that
there was a curfew. In Beverley in Yorkshire "strangers
were expected to retire indoors earlier than natives of
the town, and their hosts had to be prepared to swear to
their good behavior or else they could be shut out at nine
o'clock." (G. T. Salusbury, *Street Life in Medieval England*). Some American towns have recently made similar
ordinances; in a few cases directed against teenagers, in
others against anyone found on the streets after nine or
ten. The police may then arrest them.*

To walk without any feeling of strangeness or inse-

---

* James Schevill, who teaches at Brown University in Providence, has
written a play, *Lovecraft's Follies*, whose central character is based on
a scientist friend who worked at the Huntsville, Alabama, space center. Out walking one night, he was picked up by the local police.
They couldn't believe a "high security researcher" would be engaged
in such an activity. They put him in a state mental asylum and it
was two weeks before he was let out.

curity it is necessary to be in a community where change is moderate and considered, where the scale of streets and houses remains close and human. Forced into cars, we are suspended; our contacts are deceptive and unresponsive. People driving down Water Street often wave at people they see walking, whom they recognize, and are offended when the pedestrians do not recognize them behind the shining windshields of their cars, or do not—simply seeing the car—identify the owner. At this point I know three people who drive red Volkswagens, but should I for that reason wave at every red Volkswagen I see and feel foolish when it turns out to be driven by a stranger? So one stops looking at cars as they pass on Water Street. One stops waving. But I say hullo or good morning to other people walking, even strangers.

7

YET CONTACT is what the village is all about; we can't
avoid people. We have neither the highly charged, hap-
hazard confrontations nor the anonymity of the large
town or city. It behooves us to know people. This atmospheric imperative goes to the heads of some new
arrivals: they throw themselves into the village, head
first, without finding out the depth of the water. Some
of them hit their heads, some plunge downward forever.
The Coogans moved to School Street and within a week
were first-naming most of the people, fighting with the
others, joining the PTA and the Young Republican
Wives and taking collections for the Heart Fund. The
PTA disbanded and people went on calling them Mr.
and Mrs. Coogan and the Democrats continued to run
the village and the Coogans moved after a year. The
Merryweathers came to Water Street and did over an
old house with a fancy architect at great expense and
gave large parties every Saturday night to which people
went for a while to meet the celebrities Lois Merry-
weather brought to meet all her new friends and after a
few seasons the Merryweathers began to find the village

boring and moved on. On others, involvement creeps, though it may become just as intense. When I was in the Gold Coast in the army the tour of duty for young officers was restricted to a year, but for one or two even this was too long—they got involved. One man I knew used to dress in the evenings in a mammy-cloth, the colorful cotton robe the Africans swaddled themselves in, and then would ride his motorcycle out to a small fishing village near Tema. He had become friends with the chief of the village, and once a month while the drums sounded he would go down to the sea with his black mentor and hurl his monthly one-bottle ration of Gordon's gin into the high surf. It was to propitiate the sea god. Before his tour of duty was up he had what the medical officer called a breakdown and was shipped home to England screaming, "Africa! Africa!" In the village there are several individuals who have deliberately cast off a former existence and become villagers. From what little one knows of their carefully concealed backgrounds, successful, dominating parents lurk there —and these black sheep climb into local clothing, sometimes quite literally in the form of fishermen's work clothes, giving their business suits to the Thrift Shop and their alumni bulletins to the library; some become involved in local issues on what seems to them the side of "the common people." Once in a while, when the strain set up between upbringing and chosen role begins to tell, they throw Gordon's gin or its emotional equivalent into their own psychological surf.

Responsibilities form a reinforcing mesh into which individual lives (like wet concrete) are poured and held. Looking for evidence of mutual aid, Prince Peter Kropotkin, the anarchist and naturalist, found it most prevalent in village communities. Our own selfish needs in respect of children, books, sports, and entertainment get us involved in common attempts to answer those needs. A woman from New York who spends summers in the village said recently, "I'll look after your children today if you want. Then I can get you to drive me to Westerly station on Sunday night." This is the sort of bargaining that goes on all the time in the village—though with the perhaps crucial difference that it is rarely outspoken like that. People do things for other people and know that sooner or later things will be done for them. Our friend from the city hadn't yet learned that we take it for granted; there is no need to conduct the deal in point-blank detail. There are common denominators of help—children are one, and so are houses and boats: if you help someone lift a boat out of a garage you can count on him to help you step a mast, or assist at a launching. The other day Al Souza at one end of School Street was laying a new sidewalk, and Tony Previty from the other end of the street came to give him a hand making the forms for the concrete. A few days later when Tony Previty was painting his garage doors, down the hill came Al Souza with a brush to do some painting.

I was introduced to this interdependence quite early on School Street. I had bought a large second-hand gas stove in Norwich, and it had been dumped on the sidewalk outside the house by the trucker who brought it to the village. It weighed nearly two hundred pounds. I needed help to get it into the house and into place in the kitchen. And a week or so after this was done, one of the men who had helped me rang up while we were having dinner and asked if I could give him a hand. It turned out he wanted a hand with a hospital bed, which had to be taken from a barn to the house of a man who was dying. There we dismantled the bed the sick man usually slept in, while he sat in an armchair and coughed, and his wife looked on and thanked us. Then we set up the heavy iron hospital bed, which could be adjusted to bend and slope to fit his pained body. At the end she thanked us, and the man, who died three or four days later, said thank you, and the man who had brought me said that he was sure the sick man would be more comfortable now. Outside again, it was a night full of stars. The man who had asked me to come thanked me, apologetically. I said: Don't be silly, I was glad to be able to help, and meant it.

Children are the great joiners and levelers. We decided soon after coming to it that School Street was dangerous for children with its two-way traffic, parking on one side, and a couple of blind corners at top and bottom. Peter Tripp and I drafted a petition which Margot, my wife, then seven months pregnant, took from house to house on School Street. She thus got to know people and see what the inside of their houses looked like and let them know something about us. Everybody signed, the petition was presented to the Warden and Burgesses, the street was made one-way, and there was a pleasant sense for a while on the street that we had done something together for the best interests of everybody. There was also the satisfaction, restricted to residents of the street, of being able to shout at drivers unfamiliar with the new traffic pattern: "One Way Street!" Similarly, Margot—looking for a low-cost way of getting a preschool child off her hands in the mornings with some benefit to the child—started a cooperative nursery school, in which each young mother took a turn teaching. Dues of this group were a dollar a month, enough to purchase crayons and paste and paper—some of the "girls," as they referred to one another, wanted higher dues, because it didn't feel like a real organization without them, but the dollars mounted rapidly enough and paid for a swing as well as necessary supplies. Accommodation was found in the Sunday-school rooms of the Episcopal church. (When those quarters were eventually needed—so the vicar claimed—as an apartment for an elderly organist, the group moved on to the Congregational Sunday school, next door to the minister's office—but there the minister was deaf, and they stayed longer.) Some girls were not very good at teaching when their three-day turns came round—apparently one could tell because the children came home whiny and frustrated. Some girls had teaching experience, or had read books on the Montessori method. And some just fell into it, inventing games and songs and taking the children for long, tiring walks. Margot said it was sheer hell for the three days one taught, but worth it for the mornings of household peace in the seven or eight weeks that interspersed one's turn at teaching. She also said that in the school in good moments you could hear a bubbling, humming sound—it was all the children singing softly and privately, la-la sounds mainly but now and then a few words thrown in. In Russia they used to play songs of Leninism continuously to small children in school, but I believe they found eventually that the children shut out these irrelevant distractions by making their own songs.

The coop nursery school has had a few small dramas. One child bolted himself in the Episcopal john and then couldn't undo the bolt. The girl in charge that day lost her head and called the police. The police came and broke down the door. There was then a sizable carpenter's bill, sent on by the vestrymen, and some feeling among some young mothers that the bill could have been avoided by calling a carpenter rather than the police in the first place. One girl's son proved uncontrollable and unteachable; he spent his mornings waiting for opportunities to sock other children. So a conference was held by the other mothers. Should they ask the girl to remove her son? Should they give any reasons? Should they tell her that her son was in need of professional help? This last, they decided, was the right thing to do; but then who would tell her? It was a nasty job, and there were no volunteers, and Margot as the founder of the nursery coop found herself with the job, which she dreaded. It was interfering. It was condescending. But for the sake of all the other children and the girls who had to teach it had to be done. The girl concerned was not at all upset. She seemed relieved, Margot said—she and her husband had suspected things were wrong and had been waiting to have their fears corroborated. They welcomed a push in the right direction. They then consulted a child psychologist and in a year or so the boy was much improved; he'd also got used to his interloping baby brother by then.

In a place this size the mechanics of help remain personal; institutions tend either not to exist or to be federal, a long way away. When Bertha Stevens woke up in the hospital after an ulcer operation she couldn't afford and wasn't insured for, the first person she saw was the vicar, telling her among other things that she wasn't to worry, everything was taken care of. She said later she didn't know exactly who the people were who had subscribed to a fund to pay all those expenses, but she had a good idea. Bertha was the widow of an unsuccessful inventor and when he died she turned to making curtains and slipcovers and being a companion to wealthier widows. At the other end of the social spectrum are the Yateses. In a larger place they would be welfare cases.

Indeed, even in the village they may get some town assistance. Mr. Y is quite often drunk and unemployed, though everyone who runs a business in the town has made desperate efforts at some time to employ him. Mrs. Yates is battered, varicosed, with ten or maybe at this point eleven grubby kids, screaming, fighting, dragging themselves up. You see her pushing an old baby carriage full of laundry down to the laundromat, and Margot, who has talked to her there, says she is a friendly woman. But the point is not that (though why should we be surprised that the poor and uneducated and disadvantaged are, or can be, friendly?), but that being on the parish in Stonington and on relief in a city like New York are two quite different things. Here the Yateses are not cut off in a zone of welfare. Sometimes cleaned up a little, and sometimes not, two or three of the children are to be seen playing with Jessica Barnes, whose father is a stockbroker whose house has recently been renovated at a cost of at least fifty thousand dollars. Marcy Yates turns up with my daughter Liz at Evie Dodson's hospitable front door and is invited to go for a sail or a picnic on the Dodson yacht with some Dodson children. Old Mr. Yates, the grandfather, unshaven but unfailingly helpful and polite, still works a shift at the velvet mill and keeps a protecting eye on the whole brood. He knows the value of the house the younger Yateses live in, which sharp real estate people, seeing its exterior dilapidation, are always trying to convince the younger Yateses to sell. Where

would they go? There is no promise in the metropolis
for the Yateses. I can think of no place in the world
where they would be better off than where they are.

People pass clothes on to us and we pass them on to
other people. Thus, although we have once in a while
seen the inside of Saks and Bonwits and the Robleses
haven't, those ill-nourished children are just as liable as
ours to be wearing a chic little seven-year-old's lightly
used jacket, or a previously owned cashmere sweater.
Scarcely less personal is the Thrift Shop, staffed by volunteer ladies, and open on weekdays from one till four.
Here all sorts of clothes, furniture, and knickknacks,
given free, are resold for the benefit of the Community
Center. When people ask us enviously where we got our
antique steamer trunks, with their first-class *Berengaria*
labels, we answer: "The Thrift Shop." Charlie Storrow's
splendid tweed jacket, which his wife Anne gave him for
his last birthday, came from the Thrift Shop, as did a suit
of long underwear (bearing a Cash's name tape *Henry
Davis*) which I wear when winter sailing, and the white
Palm Beach suit I wear to summer weddings. The underwear cost fifty cents and the Palm Beach suit three dollars, which is perhaps a big enough investment when you
consider that I have been invited to only one summer
wedding since I bought the suit. The Thrift Shop is an
excellent source for ice skates and snow suits for children. It is not so good for books or china or paintings.
The books tend to be old chemistry texts, and chamber

of commerce guides to Argentine industry. Margot suspects that there is a certain stock of clothing permanently circulating around the village, going in and out of the Thrift Shop. She bases this assumption on the fact that she saw Elsie, the check-out lady in Roland's, wearing a blue flowered dress that was once hers, and that Henrietta Bowen was looking at her strangely at the Bodkins' cocktail party. "I think," said Margot, "this used to be her stole." In the spring the rich old ladies in Watch Hill clear out their houses, and connoisseurs of the Thrift Shop claim that that's the time to keep an eye on what turns up there.

It has another advantage: if you want to throw something away that has a chance of being useful to someone, it is closer than the Town Dump. But going to the dump certainly has its own fascination. The children like to go there when I take a load of old newspapers, garden debris, or accumulated cellar junk. What appeals to them may be what appeals to me: the plume of gray smoke rising above the surrounding woods like a signal, leading one to it along the Greenhaven road; the high wire gate, set in a high wire fence, stating the hours of admission and the necessity of being a resident of the town; and, once inside, the fires of blazing rubbish, the pick-up trucks backed to the edge of artificial cliffs, and a gruff, grimy dump-master, the man who runs the bulldozer and has the pickings of old bathtubs and pipe and anything that looks of value, shouting as you drive up

past a barricade of rusty oil drums—meant to guide you
to the section of the dump presently being used—and
making sure that you aren't about to dump wet garbage
in the scrap metal section, or tree limbs in with the garbage.

The garbage trucks are generally there in late mornings after they have made their rounds. This is where the
scraps and leftovers of the food we have bought at one
grocery or another all end up. (Peter Tripp had a short
period of burying his food garbage in his garden, and
achieved great lettuce productivity in the section full—
he claimed—of old cods' heads; but he now disposes of
his garbage in the same manner the rest of us do, and has
even built an elegant sidewalk shelter with a proscenium
arch for his garbage cans.) At the dump, as I've noted,
the Sandy Point seagulls drop down for quick pickings.
Their numbers increase every year in proportion to our
own increase and that of our debris. Now and then a rat
scurries across a pile of sand, planted ready for the bulldozer to cover the refuse. The dump-master fiddles with
an old truck and crane which he uses to grab scrap iron
and steel, in the shape of old stoves and kitchen sinks. He
one day caught Margot making off with a tree-pruning
implement which she'd failed to realize had been put
aside as part of his rightful spoils. I once found and successfully bore off a dozen massive hickory logs, which
blunted two saws but burned many nights in our
Franklin stove with slow heat and subtle fragrance.

Sometimes I have the same feeling of guilt leaving things at the dump as I did taking the logs away. Peter Tripp and I drove over to it one winter afternoon just before the gates were locked at five. Peter was helping me in return for a hand I'd given him moving a dory the week before. We had in the back of his old pick-up truck a refrigerator—a giant fifteen cubic feet capacity frost-free model which I'd bought as a bargain for twenty-five dollars. The trouble with this complicated machine was that it was indeed frost free: it automatically defrosted all the time. Nothing in it ever got more than luke cold. After two fifteen-dollar repair jobs (which the appliance man said were the best that could be done, no guarantees of success), it began to seem less than a bargain. My decision to scrap it was hastened by the appearance of a black slime which began to ooze from the coils at the back. Then we had to get it out of the house, which was more of a job than getting it in. Peter and I cartwheeled it out of the back door, and then, wobbling it from one corner to another, down the side yard. Bits and pieces began to fall off. There was a thin black trail. We had just got it halfway up and over the back of the truck—it was, in fact, balanced there, with me holding the bottom—when Peter remembered that he had promised to pick up Mary his wife at the library at five. He dashed off, saying he would be right back. A spider climbed out of the dusty compressor and strolled up my arm. A car of tourists stopped and looked at me, as if I were part of the historic scene hereabouts. Peter came back with Mary and caught the refrigerator just as my arms were giving way from nervous strain, and we tilted it in and drove off to the dump. There the funereal fires smoked dully. No one was about. We backed the truck to the precipitous edge of a sand embankment, feeling the sand-covered garbage squashing down beneath us, and tipped out the refrigerator. It fell on its feet, swayed slightly, but remained standing. We pulled slowly away. The refrigerator stood there in the smoky dusk, a mute memorial to our civilization. Mary gave us a smaller and older refrigerator she'd had before marrying Peter, and apart from a door handle that needs an application of epoxy and a blessing every six months, and a slight rattle in the intestines on hot summer nights, it has functioned perfectly ever since.

❧ 8 ❧

THERE IS ONE HOUSE which even at night I walk by
with a slightly quickened step. The lady who lives there
is not, as far as I know, a window-watcher, but she has—
to put it with an ambivalence she might appreciate—
a well-known tongue; when I run into her, her conven-
tional greeting is rapidly followed by a question that has
depths and dimensions below and beyond the surface
burden: Who bought such and such a house, or why
haven't the so-and-so's been seen for a long time. I suspect her imagination, and I grant her all sorts of terrible
fantasies. If she sees me walking by at night she is bound
to wonder what domestic melodrama has driven me onto
the streets, or in what sequestered nook of the village
(the old railroad station lean-to, maybe, or the back
pews of the Catholic church) I have been conducting an
assignation with—and here the mind, given so little
scope by reality, had better take wings—that hopeless
but rather sexy girl in the post office; the one who can
never remember the standard airmail rate to Europe but
whose mouth, like a mail slot, is always just, invitingly,
open. Without a doubt gossip in the village reflects the

depth of one's interest and the time one has served here. On the lips of new arrivals it seems shallow and unknowing, striking the sort of note that inspires no answers in a village veteran—in fact, has a contrary effect, jarring him into silence. But with time and acquaintance, gossip becomes more subtle. Also more profoundly forthright on occasion, as when Mary Feathers said (knowing she was unloading a brand-new surprising fact about someone known and liked): "Johnny Dickenson's leaving his wife for Marge James—he's madly in love with her. But then I don't think Marge will leave Boris, do you?"

Margery James! Very much the "last person" you would have thought of in terms of other men, other women. So hard to imagine falling in love with Margery James, a dumpy, tongue-tied girl, interested in children and boats. And yet (and the moment you thought about it there were plenty of "and yets") she was married. Presumably Boris James had fallen in love with her once, and what he, a personable young stockbroker, could do, other men might also do—might even be made aware of its possibility by the incongruous juxtaposition of Boris's charm and Marge's awkwardness. Furthermore, as someone who had lived in the village and then moved to the outskirts, Marge did seem to be always driving around as if she had lots of time on her hands. Another consideration was that Mr. Dickenson had simply seen Marge one day in the proper light and flipped. Certainly the next time I saw her she looked different. There was a delicacy in her hitherto dumpy features.

The right light is more than a handy, romantic phrase. Recent studies conducted with microorganisms suggest that an increased exposure to light intensifies the reproductive urge. I can bolster this *Scientific American* sort of note by recalling that June—the month with the longest days and most light—is the month when Gilbert White, the curate of Selbourne, watched his old Sussex tortoise beginning to make remarkable exertions: "He then walks on tiptoe, and is stirring by five in the morning." The tortoise examines all the fences, manages to get out of the garden, and then wanders to distant fields. White wrote, "The motives that impel him to undertake these rambles seem to be of the amorous kind: his fancy then becomes intent on sexual attachments, which transport him beyond his usual gravity, and induce him to forget for a time his ordinary solemn deportment." My own observations suggest that the long June days, and perhaps the moon on short June nights, may have something to do with the adventures conducted then: giggles from the driveway bushes in the closing stages of country estate cocktail parties signal the season in which other men's wives in bright summer dresses look especially ravishing. Count Kropotkin says that the Eskimos "live in families, but the family bonds are often broken; husbands and wives are often exchanged. The families, however, remain united in clans. . . . In Australia, whole clans have been seen exchanging all their wives, in order to conjure a calamity. More brotherhood is their specific against calamities." I like that "more brotherhood." Here our sense of the calamitous remains based on the integrity of the family, and it generally intervenes, better late than never, to inhibit our sense of fun. In the last few years there has been only one widely discussed case of wife-swapping, and that didn't become permanent. The quartet resumed their previous marital arrangements after putting to their respective children the question: how would you like new mummies and daddies? The children said no. They preferred those they had.

Children are not always that conservative. A more melodramatic scandal not long ago involved a group of seventeen-year-old girls and a Pied Piper who worked as the Parkinsons' handyman. The Parkinsons live on Main Street in a large vinyl-sided colonial house. Mr. Parkinson, a retired banker, is not very evident in village affairs; in fact, he is just about invisible. But he makes up for this by having a permanent handyman—the present one is a Negro—and by having a Cadillac. (Other Cadillac owners in the village are the police chief, the owner of the lumberyard, the tailor, and several of the most successful fishermen. The really rich own Fords, Mercedes, Jaguars, and Volvos.) At any rate, the Parkinsons' previous handyman had his own high visibility. He could be seen striding around the village in his dark green work suit, which on him looked like the uniform of a cavalry officer. He wore a goatee and a green beret. I was in the Thrift Shop examining a book one day when he went by and one of the volunteer ladies said, "What a dapper fellow!"

Similarly affected, the small group of teen-age girls began attending late-night shindigs thrown by the handyman in the furthest and darkest corner of the old kiln dock field, amid old dories and decaying lobster traps. Vodka, brought by the handyman, and pot, supplied by one of the young ladies, improved the atmosphere. The handyman allegedly told the girls he was Zeus reincarnated. He told them about his experiences with women. He left something to their imaginations, and when their imaginations had had a chance to provide it he found them accessible. But all good things come to an end. One girl fell out of favor with Zeus and tried to drive her car off the end of the steamboat dock. Another got pregnant and left town. There were several family crises. In the midst of the hubbub, the handyman himself suddenly disappeared, back to Mount Olympus, perhaps, or else (as an ambiguous piece in the local newspaper hinted) to a town in Arkansas where he was wanted to answer charges of bigamy.

Gossip in the village often concerns itself with money, such as absconding with church funds or going bankrupt; and it is also concerned with sanity—going mad is generally referred to as going to Norwich, which is where a mental hospital is situated. At any one time three or four people from the village will be in Norwich. For good reason, gossip rarely has to do with the several homosexual couples who live fairly inconspicuous and respected village lives. They don't flaunt their eccentricity. In return, they don't receive any particular disapprobation. As far as the village merchants are concerned, they buy food and drink like everyone else. Social people are perhaps enchanted to have their company at parties —they are "different." But the difference doesn't isolate them. Occasionally one hears of a tiff, but then matters mend, as they do in most of our heterosexual marriages. (One man, and his secretary, retired to Trinidad but most stick it out at home, like Margery and Boris James.) There are other cases where sex is more of a noticeable aggravation. One desperate woman gets drunk and walks the streets, knocks on doors, and tries to tell her own desperate story. One man, married and with children, once a year stands in his front room window and exhibits his penis to the family across the street. The first time this happened they called the police; the second time they called some friends in, more for comfort than malice; and now, when it happens, they treat it like a television program they'd rather the children didn't see. They set up diversionary activities, playing Scrabble or making fudge. "He just stands there looking sad," one child said to his parents, perhaps having learnt something about the variousness of the human animal.

The lack of privacy enforces a morality of sorts. "You can't get away with much in the village," is how one older villager put it to me. Of course, this only affects those people who care what other people think; but they seem to be the great majority. In the minority was the young girl who several years ago, after losing her fiancé in a car accident, went and laid herself down on the New Haven railroad tracks. She was seen and rescued before a train came. However, what people talked about was not the understandable act of throwing herself on the tracks but the fact that, before doing so, she took off all her clothes so that she could be run over naked.

9

PILLARS OF THE COMMUNITY: it's a phrase that comes to
mind as I walk across Wadawanuck Square and glimpse
in the dim lamplight the marble columns of the library,
a squat late-nineteenth-century structure that looks
very much like a tomb. It sits in the middle of the
square, surrounded by triangles of grass and high trees.
The drive is thick with new gravel, and the entrance
gateway is flanked with stone pillars, each supporting a
cannonball fired by the attacking British fleet in 1814.
Stone steps, divided by a polished brass rail, lead up to
the heavy, bronze-framed library doors.

The steps are a good place to sit. I sometimes rest on
them on Sunday mornings in fall while my children hunt
for chestnuts or kneel close at hand, filling with tiny
pieces of gravel the hollow pipes which support a wire
fence, put there to protect the library's foundation
shrubbery. Some of the pipes are already full of gravel;
filling them is something children seem to have done for
donkey's years. From St. Mary's, on the north side of the
square, people leave Mass, buzzing like bees leaving a
hive, girls dressed up, men in Sunday jackets and ties.

They stand talking for a minute before driving down to Frankie Keane's for the Sunday papers. (A former Episcopal vicar, finding that his visit to Frank's for the Providence *Journal* coincided with that of the Mass-leaving crowd, used to say, "Frank, Protestant *Journal*, please.") I catch some of the overflow from the church-going camaraderie as a few of those who've walked to church come past the library, returning my good mornings with an assured Sunday cheerfulness. For a moment I partake of a pleasant feeling that the village is a pond whose waters, if you immerse yourself, buoy you up. But the immersion is necessary.

My idea of myself is that of someone basically withdrawn—someone with a cool, self-preserving manner; but the village has chipped away at this conception. For several years I attended meetings of the library book committee one Monday afternoon a month. I was the only male committee member. Other members were the librarian, Mrs. Copley; Mrs. Dodge; Mrs. du Bois; Mrs. Knox; Mrs. Boatwright; and young Mrs. Storrow (whose mother-in-law, the older Mrs. Storrow, presided over the Historical Society archives in the library basement). During my early days on the book committee Mrs. Dodge was the senior member. She subscribed to English literary magazines and handed them on to the library, together with large quantities of detective novels. An hour before the meeting she would phone the librarian to find out if any of the other members had a cold; if they had, she wouldn't come. It was perhaps Mrs. Dodge's great-grandfather, Benjamin Sheffield Cutler, who handed on to her this strong survival instinct. Serving on the ship *Volunteer*, he once landed on an island off the South American coast and there, cooking food, was caught in a grass fire and roasted all over. The other "resourceful New Englanders" (as Mrs. Dodge called them) caught some penguins, split them open, and bound them round the burned body of young Cutler. They replaced these dressings with fresh ones every twenty-four hours. In ten days the injured man began to grow a new skin, and in a month he was walking again. Mrs. Dodge said that he lived to be a hale old man.

In picking books the committee first of all took for granted the fact that a demand for entertainment existed and must be satisfied. For this, in the form of light novels or heavy, pseudo-documentary fictions, a source fortunately existed: a book rental service, which every month supplied ten books by mail and after a few months took them back again. This, and book club subscriptions, provided "best-sellers" and ensured that the library shelves weren't crammed with purchased works of transient interest. It allowed members of the book committee to concentrate on what they considered to be books worth debate. The members usually came to the monthly meeting armed with a list of books, and a crop of clippings to support their choices. Mrs. du Bois would want Georgette Heyer's latest Regency romance, but she now and then surprised us by saying, "Now what has Henry Miller written recently?"—on one occasion asking the librarian (for she was a bit tottery on her feet herself) to go to the card catalogue to see if the library had *Black Spring*. Henry Miller wrote the sort of books the other members thought—diffidently—we might perhaps keep one of, in a locked cupboard, and I thought we mightn't really need at all—except perhaps as a historical example, and then certainly on an open shelf.

Mrs. Boatwright, active in state politics, would deliver her list crisply, rarely pausing for remarks of approval or disapproval, but simply handing the paper after she'd finished to Mrs. Copley—there was a slight suggestion that Mrs. Copley could get busy copying down the titles in her official list of books to order; there was no need for debate. Mrs. Knox went more slowly and less artfully, often leaving a doubt-filled pause after one of her proposals—"Now, we haven't had a book about India recently, have we?" This gave Mrs. Boatwright the chance to say, "Oh, Ann, we have four of them, and I bet they never go out, do they, Rita?" (As with a teenage girl, how often it gets asked out is a measure of a book's popularity.) Rita Copley would have to admit that they didn't go out—India didn't seem to be people's cup of tea this year. No one was reading the Afro-American books that had been ordered, either. Mrs. Knox liked books on India, wild animals, and good counsel about marriage and family planning, which embarrassed young Mrs. Storrow, who was pregnant. And while Mrs. Boatwright and I had a tacit bargain whereby we exchanged loud approval for several of each other's choices, Mrs. Knox never seemed to have come to any such arrangement, or at that point to have realized that one might be necessary. The result was sometimes a contagious silence after she'd finished, hardly dissipated when she said, "Oh, I suppose none of you like my books again this month." But now, perhaps because of her independent intransigence, she is library president.

Young Mrs. Storrow had definitely thought of one book "we surely ought to have," and which would be in demand—memoirs of a New England girlhood, or a sexy avant-garde Brazilian novel. They would go down well. I, as the only man, was given a certain freedom with books about the sea, or sports, but otherwise I had no more rights than anyone else. So my tactics varied. Sometimes I came fully prepared, having put some thought into what I might reply when I suggested a volume of marvelous short stories by J.C. or J.U., and one of my fellow committee members would say, "Oh, but no one reads short stories." No one reads short stories partly because in libraries books of them get put on shelves marked "Short Stories." Readers need tempting to pick them up, since they know they are going to be forced to change loyalties, get identified and unidentified with characters fairly often, and switch moods faster than they might fancy when putting their feet up for a long read. Coming as they do in strong, intense bursts, good for reading in planes or trains, perhaps short stories should be put on shelves marked "Travel Reading" or "Journeys."

Some months I went less prepared and heard myself making gusty statements: "P. G. Wodehouse writes better English than anyone living, and we must have . . ." Now and then the concern behind these speeches got across, or the ladies took pity on me, thinking, "Well, we must keep him happy, he's our only man." But sometimes they were perfectly cool to my recommendation —or so I thought at the time, not realizing that a seed had been planted and would later flower. No, no, they said unanimously in January, a history of Art Nouveau for twenty-five dollars! Much too much. And who would read it? In March Mrs. Copley said, "I see there's a new volume out on Art Nouveau" and Mrs. Boatwright would say, "You know, our art section is very weak. Roy Lichtenstein was telling a class at Dorsey's [her daughter's] school that . . ." And young Mrs. Storrow, lovely girl, would add, "Oh yes, do let's have Art Nouveau."

Called the "free library," it is supported by private funds—by endowments and annual gifts, and by five-hundred-dollar annual grants from the town and the village. Book overdue charges of two cents a day go into the petty cash box—it has been stolen twice by someone, presumed to be a young lad (Dickens: "Boys is wicked"), who broke in through one of the cellar windows. The new wing at the rear, built with funds provided in Dr. Paffard's will, has a large basement room used by the Village Improvement Association and other local groups for their general meetings. Upstairs is the children's section, where in the winter on Saturday mornings the librarian and volunteers conduct a children's story hour—a light, sunny room, full of the green of trees in summer or the white of snow in winter. But I prefer the old building. Within, it is less like a tomb than a Victorian conservatory with most of the glass blacked out. You can sit in a shady corner with *Country Life* or *Scientific American*. A balcony, iron-railed, runs around three of the walls, and is reached by a semi-spiral staircase. Up there are history, plays, and poems, for which I would, if I had to, forgo all the novels downstairs. You have to duck your head under some of the beams, which are ornately molded, and by turning on with a pull cord the incongruous fluorescent light by each set of shelves, you expect to see (and are somewhat disappointed not to see) a gargoyle at each joint and corner.

The balcony is also a good place for—literally—eavesdropping. People coming in have no idea you are up there, thumbing through Carl van Doren's *Secret History of the American Revolution* or dreaming about a musical based on the career of Major André. You are brought to realize that a librarian is a confessor for some —in the way that bank managers and barbers and doc-

tors may also be. The library is a place where the most
seemingly tolerant people can be opinionated, can unload
prejudices, denounce the rich, criticize the poor, crack
an anti-Semitic joke or two, complain about filth in
modern literature and suggest that no one ever writes
anything serious anymore, and then, after a few minutes'
browsing, walk out with a very funny, very dirty novel
written by a Jew who is probably, by now, a millionaire.
Meanwhile the librarian, a lady of immaculate patience
and understanding, puts the library ticket into the dating
machine and almost smiles.

⤝ 10 ⤞

THE CANNONBALLS ARE BLACK, round, and a little pock-marked. It is hard to think of them whistling over the village and splintering through the clapboards of a house, or even thudding into a vegetable patch or herb garden. One might say, sentimentally, it was hard to think of them being fired in anger, except that there was indeed very little anger on the part of those who ordered them to be fired. They were an expression of policy.

Sir, I have the honour to send you, for the information of my Lords Commissioners of the Admiralty, a dispatch which I have this day received from the Honourable Rear Admiral Hotham acquainting me of the result of an attack which he had directed to be made upon the Town of Stonington by part of the Division of His Majesty's Ships under his orders.

So wrote Vice Admiral Alexander Cochrane from his flagship *Surprize* in the Patuxent River on August 29, 1814. A few weeks before, he had received word from Rear Admiral Hotham, from his flagship *Superb* off Gardiner's Island:

(83)

Sir, His Majesty's Ship *Ramilles* and the *Terror* Bomb[ship] having joined me at this anchorage on the 7th instant, and being informed by the officers who had commanded here, that the Town of Stonington has been conspicuous for preparing and harbouring torpedoes, and giving assistance to the insidious attempts of the Enemy at the destruction of His Majesty's Ships employed off New London, it appeared to be more deserving of the visitation prescribed in your Order of the 18th Ultimo, than any other place on this part of the Coast. . . . I therefore directed Sir Thomas Hardy on the 8th Instant, to take the direction of such an attack on the Town, with the Ships and Vessels named in the margin,

Ramilles
Pactolus
Dispatch
Terror—Bomb

with a view of destroying it by their fire, as he might find practicable, conformably to your order alluded to; and enclosed I have the honour to transmit to you an extract of the report of the execution of it, with a return of the casualties on board the Dispatch on the occasion. The destruction of the Town has not been as complete as could have been wished.

And from Hardy:

On the evening of the 11th I directed Captain Sheridan to throw a few more shells and Carcasses into the Town, which not setting the Houses on fire as expected, I this morning anchored the Ramilles and Pactolus as near as we could place them to the Shore, from the shallowness of the water, and both Ships fired several broadsides at the Town, which was very much damaged, altho' from the houses being constructed of wood, none were seen to fall.

This was in the last year of the last Anglo-American war. England across the ocean was winding up its long struggle to free Europe of Napoleon and protect its mercantile world hegemony. On this distant Atlantic flank, a rigorous naval blockade had proved to be the most effective way of minimizing the nuisance the Americans were making of themselves. The prime cause of the subsidiary conflict had been the impressment into the British navy of American seamen. Even so, it wasn't a very popular war, especially in New England, whose trade suffered. But in time the blockade became infuriating. The British fleet hung along the coast in all seasons and all weathers, displaying unlauded seamanship of high skill in the process, occasionally landing a party to buy cattle at the going rate, or chasing a schooner which tried to make a run for it. It was a war in which each side treated the other with ceremony. Officers served as pallbearers at the burial of the fallen foe. A young English midshipman, interred at Stonington with full honors, had been killed while boarding a privateer disguised as a merchantman. Earlier, ten British seamen and an officer were killed when they boarded a schooner carrying not only provisions but a charge of dynamite, planted to blow up for the occasion—one form of "torpedo" or "insidious attempt" that aggravated the British. In July, 1813, a mysterious diving machine was seen off New London, according to the *Gentleman's Magazine* "the invention of a gentleman [who else?] living at Norwich," the town further up the Thames River from New London. The British regarded these innovations as not cricket. There is also reason to believe that the visitation—prescribed by Henry Hotham for Stonington as the "more deserving" place—was the final reaction to unexpected American assaults on British settlements across the Canadian border.

Certainly Hardy himself failed to give the impression that he had his heart in it. Nelson said: "I never knew Hardy wrong upon any professional subject." Along the New England coast, Hardy had the reputation of being a humane and just officer, interested only in keeping Decatur and his ships bottled up in the Thames and in preventing privateers from operating. His squadron arrived off Stonington on August 9, a Tuesday, the weather (according to the log of the *Ramilles*) moderate and cloudy to begin with, though later on, when a flag of truce was sent ashore, it was "light airs and fine." Hardy's message gave the inhabitants an hour to get themselves and their belongings out of town, but he then allowed three hours to pass. In the village of a hundred tightly packed wooden houses there was consternation but no great panic. The old, the sick, and noncombatants left for neighboring farms. Valuable possessions were carted off, buried in gardens, or lowered into wells. One old lady who didn't leave was Hilda Hull; attended by her grand-daughter, she was dying of consumption in a house near the defenders' battery. This was two eighteen-pounders and one six-pounder behind a breastwork four feet high.

The battle began that first evening at eight when the British fired shells, carcasses, and Congreve rockets into the town. The defenders fired back, as it got dark aiming at the British ships when they were illuminated by rocket glare. And so it went on fitfully through Wednesday, Thursday, and Friday while the weather stayed fine. The British bombardment killed two horses, wounded three men, and set fire to a number of houses. In all forty houses were damaged, eight to ten "essentially so," and two or three ruined. Mrs. Hull died on Wednesday morning and was buried. The British sloop *Dispatch* was hit by the well-directed fire from the village, and lost two men killed and twelve wounded. This was the account of a Nantucket man who a few days later boarded one of the British ships to redeem his confiscated boat. Hardy's report confirms the number of casualties.

The gunner in charge of the Stonington battery was a man from Mystic, five miles away. Jeremiah Holmes had learned the gunnery trade during an enforced three-year service in the Royal Navy, and must have taken pleasure in demonstrating to the British how well he had mastered their skill. At one point the ammunition ran out and the cannons were spiked, but more shot and powder arrived from a cache uncovered at the Swan tavern; the vent of one of the eighteen-pounders was drilled out again so that the gun could go back into action. At another point a man called John Miner was badly burned in the face by a premature discharge. Frederick Denison was slightly wounded in the knee by a flying rock fragment (he died later that fall, though no one said whether this injury was to blame). Several times flags of truce went back and forth, as the village magistrates tried to convey to Captain Hardy both their strong disapproval of what he was doing to their town and their hope— proudly enough stated—that he would cease and desist. They assured him no torpedoes were being fitted out here. (In 1964 Jeremiah Holmes's great-grandson recalled that the master-gunner had a torpedo stored in his cellar.) Hardy was upset as well about the situation of the wife of the former British consul in New London, Mrs. James Stewart, and demanded that she and her children be sent aboard the *Ramilles*. The village fathers said this was out of their power—and later wondered a trifle maliciously why Captain Hardy had this sudden need for Mrs. Stewart. Hardy, at any rate, took the opportunity of one of these exchanges to point out to them in his cabin the couch on which Lord Nelson had died.

There were long lulls between British bombardments. In the village, the regional home guard, the militia, finally arrived in strength and insured the place against a British landing. They were kept busy putting out fires. On Friday afternoon Hardy and his fleet hauled away from the town. In the *Ramilles* log one reads:

> *Moderate and fine weather*
> *Water remaining 170 tuns*
> *2 pm Employed clearing Ship for sea*
> *at 2.30 weighed and dropped down*
> *3 WSW Boats ahead sounding at 4 ditto weather.*
> *Water shoaling came to with the Best*
> *Bower in 7 fathoms. sent boats to Buoy*
> *the channel. At 6 light breezes and fine*

Next morning at three thirty, with light breezes and clear, the *Ramilles* made sail and with the other vessels in the fleet proceeded slowly down Fishers Island Sound, not then the well-buoyed passage it is now, but a maze of unmarked rocks and shoals. The *Ramilles* ran aground. Its crew spent the next ten hours carrying out anchor cables, pumping overboard the water stored forward, moving guns and shot from the bows to the stern, putting anchors down and winching them up again, and finally kedging off into deeper water. In the midst of this procedure another truce party turned up from Stonington. Afterwards, the ship continued about the normal business of the blockade: getting provisions, bullocks, and sheep from a schooner and distributing these supplies to the other vessels; sending armed boats to chase several sailing craft which appeared in the mouth of the Mystic River; cutting off a section of the best anchor cable where it had chafed on rocky ground; and detailing boats to row guard. The log of the *Ramilles* notes the times when the men were employed washing and scrubbing their clothes, and, with a poignant lack of explanation, adds that at two thirty one morning "fell overboard and was drowned Jas. Shelden."

DESPITE THE LACK of general patriotic sentiment (Connecticut, for instance, wouldn't allow its militia to serve outside the state), the British attacks on shipping and on small towns such as Stonington had, as Mahan pointed out, the eventual effect of bringing the meaning of war close home to the consciousness of the American people —though perhaps one can better say Wareham people or Pettipaug people or Stonington people. Stonington was now bathed with the light of history. Violence had waved its melodramatic hand over the place, and the village would never be the same again. Something singular had happened to it. The event was immediately glossed and glorified, in local talk and in ballads such as that by Philip Freneau: "It cost the King ten thousand pounds to have a go at Stonington." In Congress General Root declared, "There was one achievement that sheds lustre on the American character, the defence of Stonington. . . . It was not rivalled by the defence of the Sandusky, the attempt at Niagara, or the victories of Erie and Champlain." And though later historians have been a little less confident of the battle's quality—one of them finding the chief interest of the Battle of Stonington in the great difference between the accounts of the fights as rendered by either side—in Stonington it became a moment to be celebrated. On the hundredth anniversary in 1914 there was a parade of fifteen fire companies, a historical pageant, motorboat races and speeches. "When our forefathers defended this place against the attacks of the British it was not simply for the sake of their own families and their immediate descendants," said Dean Randall of Brown University, great-grandson of Colonel Randall, the militia commander. Perhaps so, but even if the motives of the defenders were neither broader nor nobler, nothing less than immediate, for their sakes and the sake of their village, it made Stonington a defended site: a particular place particular men had risked their lives for.

The cannons sit now in the square and children play on them. Yet something they remind us of has been taken out of our hands since the Treaty of Ghent was signed in December, 1814, ending that war, and Hardy was made a Knight Commander of the Bath. Obscure treaties now defend us, and intricate weapons in underground silos. Hot lines pass messages way over our heads; no local magistrates carry flags of truce. We have no battery ramparts, no watchtowers or beacons, except far off in the Canadian tundra and in offices where men watch electronic data-processing machines. Young men from School Street depart to fight in a war they feel less connection with than their forefathers felt with the war of 1812. Patriotic bumper stickers are rare enough in Stonington, perhaps because people realize there is no proper way to nail a flag to a mast any more, the way Jeremiah Holmes is said to have done that August.

Because of this, I find that I look almost with affection at the nuclear submarines, carrying Poseidon missiles, as they leave and enter New London harbor. They are ships, crewed by men, and black and dangerous as they seem going down the Thames and across the Sound, they are susceptible to contact and understanding. I know men who help build them, and men who sail in them. They are not only tangible but vulnerable. There are several young women in the village whose husbands went down on the USS *Scorpion.*

My friend Yale Lewis served for several years on a sub based in New London. He would be at sea for two or three months and then home in the village for a month, ferreting the skunks from under his house on Gold Street. I had dinner with him one night aboard his submarine, which was an older, diesel- and electric-powered boat. I was surprised to see how many things in the sub were still done by hand—there were many valves with big bronze knobs that had to be turned, and all sorts of manual levers. As I passed close to one set of levers, Yale said urgently, "Hey, don't lean against them!" For dinner we sat at one end of a little table in a sort of aircraft-interior space and ate broiled chicken, creamy mashed potatoes, peas, and a huge serving of pink ice cream that tasted like tooth paste. At the other end of the table, a few feet away, were three officers who clearly had long practice in pretending other people weren't there, gloomily attempting to balance the ship's books. There seemed to be a number of items they were having trouble adjusting and accounting for. It made me think of the notes made in the *Ramilles* log in regard to the tons of water hastily disposed of to refloat the ship, and of the fathoms of anchor cable that they had had to chop away.

11

IN SUMMER the village seems smaller and more intense than it does the rest of the year. The population suddenly increases with summer residents and summer visitors. For a week or so in early June the permanent villagers feel particularly oppressed and irritated. They duck indoors at the sound of city people shouting to one another in the streets. City people have louder voices, used to being raised above the noise of sanitation trucks, air conditioners, and jackhammers, and they appear to have none of our sensibilities about the outdoors. Most of the villagers are embarrassed to carry on a conversation in a tone which all the neighbors could hear. The invasion of traffic into our territory is another unsettling thing. I hear myself abruptly abandoning my own sensibilities and screaming at a high-school kid, dragging up Water Street in a two-year-old Mustang with beefed-up rear springs, *"SLOW DOWN!"* Peering groggily from huge station wagons, Midwestern families drive dangerously the wrong way up Water Street, a one-way street which local pedestrians are conditioned to crossing after looking only one way. There is even less parking room than usual on School Street, and feeling more than ever engulfed in megalopolis, we drive around the block looking for a space, snarling at the sight of New York or California license plates. Some local people jet off to Europe, or go to stay with relatives in Vermont. They then rent their houses at seasonally inflated prices, and we are jealous of the new arrivals from the city who can afford such rents. It takes us nearly a month to get used to them.

The adjustment process is well lubricated. July swims forward with cocktail parties, dances, dinners, picnics, and poker games. Summer people are energetic about putting down immediate roots. The phone rings all the time and invitations fly back and forth. By August 1, natives with boats flee on long cruises, or at least, saying they are going on long cruises, go and anchor off the western breakwater. Margot by then has taken to getting up at seven thirty and calling people we scarcely know to say thank you for the invitation, we're sorry we can't come. Even if we want to we often can't because babysitters are in short supply and hard to hold on to. Year-round residents are supposed to be understanding when their hitherto dutiful young child-minder says "Do you mind if I sit for the Perkinses' house-guests this weekend?" How can they deny the girl the chance to better herself by looking after a pair of chic children, watch color television, and come back later on with sulky notions of raising her price to a dollar an hour?

Walking past the Macphersons' late at night I hear the sounds of highly amplified rock music, and although I always have a marvelous time at the Macphersons' parties and think Mr. Macpherson is a very good sort and Mrs. Macpherson is nifty, I for a moment resent them and all the vivid, knowledgable people that congregate around them. The summer imposes this love-hate thing with *that* and *them*. Some are fair-weather friends. How lucky you are to live here all the time, they say, while packing up to go back on or just after Labor Day to well-paying city jobs from which (they also say) they will at some point retire and come to live here year-round.

The intensity of things is enhanced by doldrum weather. It sometimes closes in from mid-June to early August, enshrouding the whole tight-packed peninsula with warm, opaque moisture. The water seems closer on all sides. On such calm, foggy days you can hear all the sounds of the water, diesels thumping on the fishing draggers, outboards, and people calling to one another over the noise of outboards: "Harry says there's three feet of water in here. What d'ya think, Al?" and Al yelling back, "Watch out, Harry, I can see the rocks!" There are foghorns, and the bell buoy off the outer breakwater, and the slap of flag halliards on the aluminum flagpole put up on the Point by the Chamber of Commerce to commemorate the glorious victory of August, 1814. The collection box installed at the base for

contributions toward the still undefrayed cost occasionally gets stolen, perhaps by the same thieves who recently unbolted the change machine from a wall in the
laundromat. Even on a foggy day cars drive down to the
Point for the view of the close-at-hand fog-covered
rocks. Off the Wadawanuck Club dock you can hear the
voice of the junior sailing instructor: "George, if you
can't act like a good sport and quit you'd better not
show up here again." Some invisible small boy is loudly
protesting George for hitting him amidships, and further
off, several other children are yelling that they are lost.

The club is a sixty-year-old summer institution (a recent move to make it year-round was defeated by a
healthy majority of members). It stands at the head of
the harbor, squashed up against the New Haven railroad
tracks—though certainly on the *right* side of them—
with a small single-story clubhouse, offering several
porches, a large indoor room, cloakrooms, and kitchen.
Outside are changing rooms, a short stretch of lawn, and
six tennis courts. At low tide the beach is mostly made
up of small, slimy rocks; at high tide a protective net
does an imperfect job of keeping out weeds, eel grass,
and whatever comes up-harbor on the flood. There are
not only sailing but swimming lessons for children, tennis tournaments, and races every Saturday afternoon in a
fleet of unhandy fiberglass boats chosen as an uncostly
compromise between a racing boat, a daysailer, and a
trainer that didn't need much maintenance—ignoring the

facts that children would be far better off learning to sail in a boat that was fun, capsizable, and needed looking after. Young mothers find the club beach a useful place on summer afternoons to deposit their children, while they sun themselves and exchange notes on husbands, houseguests, and housewifery. Older matrons on the porch eating chef's salads try to ignore the children but now and then get upset with the pre-teen noise, or the sight of a baby with no clothes on. On Thursday evenings there are cook-outs, originally intended as family picnics en masse but now—perhaps expressing an unconscious need of the older adults to forget such familial responsibility—more drunk-in than cook-out. Parents with small children stay at home, protecting their impressionable young from the sight of the senior citizens weaving happily through the charcoal smoke. There are three or four black-tie dances during the season, and on Labor Day a presentation of cups and prizes.

As country clubs or yacht clubs go, the Wadawanuck is not especially fancy. The dues are moderate—ranging roughly from a hundred to two hundred dollars a year. It is a great deal easier, in some ways, to belong to it and not make much use of it than it is not to belong, in which case one may find oneself developing an irritating chip on the shoulder about the place and its members. How does one get in? People who want to join the club don't want to tell too many people about their ambition in case they don't make it. Most seem to embark on the matter hesitantly, saying confidentially to a friendly member: "Now, tell me about the club . . ." A few may ask bluntly, as if money were all that might hold them back, "What are the dues?" And in reply most members hem and haw a little, going on about the long waiting list and asking at the right time of year and making sure you have the right people sponsoring your entry.

In a somewhat postliterate age, it is curious that the mechanics of the situation involve so much letter-writing. A proposer writes a letter, and so does a seconder, and so do three or four other people. They are presumed to say that the individual or family being sponsored is charming, well mannered, well educated, and interesting. It helps that they are permanently resident in Stonington or have intentions to be so. Names of wives, children, schools, colleges, jobs are attached, together with some indication of sailing or tennis ability. Intelligence doesn't seem to be a criterion. Apparently it doesn't do any harm if everyone writes the same letter. The letters are addressed to the Chairman of the Admissions Committee. (It seems to me there might be a party game in writing to such a committee letters which, on the surface, highly recommended someone and between the lines did just the opposite.) In the late winter the proposer gives a party at which the intending member and wife are introduced to a group of crucial club people—not inviting those whom the would-be member has

(99)

rubbed the wrong way. Here, clearly, the would-be member and spouse should make a good and honest impression, not talking opinionatedly or being too hail-fellow. Of course, allowance is made for genuine lapses. At a tea given by a proposer's wife to introduce one young matron to the female element of the club presidium, the young woman dropped her cake on the Persian carpet, spilled her tea in her saucer, and—excusing herself hurriedly—only just made it to the toilet to throw up. But she was four months pregnant, and excusable. On the other hand, certain features of a person which are too evidently characteristic may be damning—a tone of voice is enough.

Some people who aren't members accuse club members of prejudice, but I suspect that prejudice within the club exists in about the same proportions as it does without. Perhaps because one expects it, it is more obviously there. There are no Negro members—a condition that reflects a deficiency in the local population. Jewish members have had to be fought for, and so have poor intellectuals and Frenchmen. Plump, well-invested ladies, mindful of which schools their daughters went to and where their clothes were bought, tend to be intolerant of anything that looks like rocking the Mayflower, and it isn't surprising to find every once in a while that, say, one in ten of them is anti-Semitic. One such dowager, describing the long-haired beatnik boy brought home by an adored granddaughter, said to me, "Well, at least his name wasn't Rosenberg." It took me a few seconds to catch on. I know several people called Rosenberg, and had never thought of them as having a typical name, as if one were to say, damning all Anglo-Saxons, "Well, at least his name wasn't Smith." In fact, one Rosenberg I know had to put up with a long reminiscence of consular life in Cairo from a club lady, who suddenly concluded she was being tactless and—tactlessly—apologized. "Oh, don't worry," said Rosenberg, an archeologist, "some of my best friends are Egyptians."

My own intolerance is aroused by spoiled teenage boys in overpowered outboard boats charging around the harbor, making waves which swamp dinghies, causing cruising boats to roll on their moorings, and filling the air with clouds of offensive blue exhaust. I also get annoyed by the legalistic approach to small-boat racing that detracts from the pleasure of the Saturday afternoon races —which often seem to be won on the floor of the clubhouse in the after-the-race protest meeting. A French girl once said to me, "Life is desperate but not serious." It is a remark few people in the club would have made, life for them being very serious but rarely desperate.

. . .

❧❧❧

Sitting on the rocks at the Point on a summer night, with a fog thick enough to hide the navigation lights on the buoys and beacons, and the air so still there is no slap of halliards against the flagpole, it is possible to think of earlier arrivals. I sometimes imagine a longship snaking around Napatree, the oars pulling smoothly, the lookout keeping an eye on the edge of the beach. A stone, supposedly with runic inscriptions, was found up at Wequetequock, a few miles from the village, in the nineteenth century. I have a feeling that the Vikings were the first summer people here. In *The King's Mirror*, a book of advice written by a Norseman for his son, one reads: "Make your ship good to look upon, then skillful men will come, and the ship will be well manned. Make your ship ready for the sea when the summer starts, and navigate in the best part of the summer, and always have reliable ropes in your ship, and do not stay on the sea in the autumn if you can help it." Up in the woods behind Old Mystic there are curious semi-underground shelters, little vaults roofed over with flat stones, for which no one seems to have an explanation. Were they fortified summer houses? Certainly, if the Vikings did get here, coasting down from their winter quarters in Iceland and

Greenland, one suspects one understands what sensations of outrage, what feelings of their territory being violated, were felt by the natives—the Skraelings, as the Vikings called them—perched on this peninsula. Wadawonnet was the name the Indians used to call it, at least as it was recorded in the will of William Cheeseborough in 1667. But unlike the Northmen, Mr. Cheeseborough came to stay. In his will he left the long point of land which is now the village to his sons.

Behind my right shoulder as I sit on the rocks the water laps on du Bois beach, a small stretch of sand given to the Village Improvement Association by a philanthropic citizen and run by that association for the benefit of Stonington people. On summer mornings buses haul in children from other sections of the town for swimming lessons. The "town" includes rural sections, country roads along which suburban development is taking place, as well as the east half of the village of Mystic, and Pawcatuck, which is the western, mostly residential part of Westerly, Rhode Island. The town population—including the eighteen hundred or so people who live in the village—is roughly fourteen thousand. A two-dollar fee gives town and village families the right to use the beach. There is a lifeguard, and a float to swim out to and sit on. On holidays and weekends there is also a policeman who attempts to preserve the beach for townspeople and their friends, sending on anglers, campers, and sea-hungry inlanders to the extensive beaches of

Rhode Island. One hot Labor Day a few years ago this policeman, a plump, elderly supernumerary, had his weary attention drawn to a young man, bearded and a bit scruffy, who was doing something strange under a towel.

"What's going on there?" said the policeman, lunging forward.

"What's that?" said the young man, who was an English painter, and who was trying to get his bathing suit on under a towel, the way they do on British beaches, squirming in the sand, sticking out one leg and then the other, all the while trying to keep the towel in place.

"What's this funny business?" said the officer, meaning by that portmanteau question, Why is the young man against haircuts, motherhood, decency, and the town of Stonington. "Where's your beach card?"

"What beach card?"

From this point it was downhill. As all young Europeans are supposed to know, all American policemen are protofascists. As all American policemen allegedly are sure, all young long-haired artists from outa-town are trying to pull some funny business. These two became such caricatures. The artist got surly and the cop got tough. The artist didn't have a beach card but he was staying, he said, with the Hales, who did. Unfortunately he couldn't remember the name of the street the Hales were living on. Anyway, why should he remember? He was arrested for indecent exposure and hauled off to the lockup. It was late that night before the Hales retrieved him, after assuring a judge that he really was a house guest and after the judge—a cosmopolitan type—had explained to the policeman that Europeans often changed on their beaches and after the policeman had declared, maybe so, but at four in the afternoon on Labor Day he wasn't about to have the mickey taken out of him by an out-of-town hippie.

No doubt of it, there is a very strong and natural urge to undress that affects us on beaches. My two smallest daughters arrive at the water's edge and immediately start divesting themselves of all clothes, pants, bathing suits. The sea is our ancient element, in which we ought to be free again. We were sitting one August afternoon on Sandy Point, the old northern spit of Napatree which was turned into a long, sandy island by the 1938 hurricane. The island, privately owned by the Gildersleeve family, is now leased by the Stonington Community Center, but at the time the Gildersleeves leased most of it for a reasonable sum to the Sandy Point Association, a village organization which collected ten dollars a season for family memberships, patroled the island, and did a half-hearted job of keeping it unlittered. The Gildersleeves have a private section, which the Association located in its annual broadsheet, and which generally seemed to be marked, on the ground, in quite another part of the island. I'm never quite sure where it is. In any event, on this particular summer afternoon we were sitting on the west-facing beach, halfway along the island. We had some friends called Hawkins with us from Washington. A small motorboat pulled in to the beach with what I thought was little respect for the fact that we were right there and the rest of the beach was empty. A tall, middle-aged man got out and planted an anchor. He said, "Do you mind if I swim here?"

Assuming he hadn't a membership card as we had, I said, doing a good deed, "No, go ahead. Be our guest."

But the intruder didn't seem aware of my nice intentions. He said, "I mean swim right here. In the nude."

I didn't know what to say to that. But Jane Hawkins, a broad-minded mother, called out, "Well, in that case why don't you go down the beach a way so we don't have to stare at you?"

The man said: "It happens to be my beach."

We gathered our belongings together. We trudged away down the beach, putting several hundred yards between ourselves and Mr. Gildersleeve, who had already plunged into the water, and was bobbing happily up and down like a pale gray seal.

❦

Sandy Point is one of the best things about the village. It is a feature of life that I remember when I am away from Stonington. It is a good thing that it can be reached only by boat, and sailing there, mostly without an engine, we perhaps prize it even more than those who get there swiftly. For the moment, too, a tripartite balance is precariously kept between private owner, semi-public association, and the island's natural life. The ridge of dunes is where hundreds of gulls live—it is their place, and they protect it with angry noise and threatening dives against anyone who intrudes. The sea waves break on the steeper western beach, while on the sheltered bay side to the east, low tide bares a flat expanse of dark sand and mud, the home of horseshoe crabs and clams. Water rats scurry at night for the debris of picnics. And people perch on the edge of the island, watching their boats and anchor lines and their children splashing and digging, sometimes with their barbecue stoves and beach umbrellas seeming to establish a miniature street, or village— each with his own patch of ground, waving or calling to friends but not imposing on one another. Sandy Point is a place where one goes to be by oneself, or with one's family, away from the summer hubbub. We take our close friends there as a way of honoring them, and of showing them how lucky we are.

12

PART OF THE SUMMER population explosion is caused by relatives, with whom the blessings of a seaside village have to be shared. In July and August the density of certain homes becomes high indeed. Walking past I hear a snatch or two—"Jesus, Mom, I've had enough"—that indicate generation gaps in need of resetting. There are backfires and ill-timed explosions. Marriages crack like cylinder blocks and shatter under the burden of an extra child or two, nephews and nieces left by brothers and sisters. There are suddenly stepchildren to stay for a month, offspring from marriages formerly dissolved. One August our friends the Hillses, on nearby Quiambaug Cove, were putting up Penney Hills's brother and his wife, together with their four small boys, French nursemaid, two elderly French ladies who dropped by for five days, and (when the ladies left) the wife's sister and baby. Although they had been looking forward to the visit all spring, and had made extensive plans for joint trips and entertainment, the Hillses caved in under the sudden pressure of people. The Hillses' children fled to their grandparents' house. Rust and Penney chartered a boat for two weeks and went off on it, saving (so Rust said) their marriage. At the Tripps', next door to me, Mary's daughter Dana came to stay, bringing husband Harl and three children. An old friend of the family sent a son for a few weeks, saying "maybe he can help Peter with his boat." And at weekends Mary's second daughter, Sharon, came down from Providence with her husband and baby. Fortunately Peter's son Nat was away in the army and not due home for a year. Peter himself spent a lot of time in his lettuce patch, looking like Mr. McGregor in wait for Peter Rabbit.

The pressures are not only emotional. Henry Chapin correctly prophesied in April that his son-in-law Rust Hills—then claiming to be looking forward to a big family summer—would not only be blowing his stack by the end of July but would be experiencing an acute water shortage. The Hillses' well ran dry by mid-August. On School Street, where we have plenty of mains water (although at the highest price in Connecticut), the problem was how to get rid of the water once it had been used. The sewer blockage first made itself felt in Peter's cellar. The previous owner of Peter's house had done a great deal of his own plumbing, and there were eccentricities in the installation which caused Peter (whose house in fact was not the lowest on the blocked line) to be the first to get a whiff of things. The trouble was put down to roots that had broken into his pipe as it passed under his garden on the way to the harbor. The Roto-Rooter man, whose interest in roots may have affected his diagnosis of the situation, arrived and cleared one hundred feet of line at a charge of forty-two dollars. Peter's line joins several other lines, including mine, well within that length, but since the Roto-Rooter man charged by the hundred feet he cleared exactly that length and no farther. The next day Doris Lambrecht, who lives in the cottage on the other side of Peter's house, called to Margot across the intervening garden with a voice that still has a base of clear Cockney, though she has been in America for twenty years: "Mrs. Byeley, Mrs. Byeley, the sewer's backed up all over hour yard. Will you please not flush your toilet for a while?"

It was a hot day. Peter, smartly, had gone off for a week's sailing secure in the knowledge that the Roto-Rooter man had done his stuff. At lunch time we were still not flushing. Mary had managed to telephone the Roto-Rooter man but he disclaimed all responsibility except for the first hundred feet; he didn't know what other lines joined the main stem; it was quite likely the obstruction had merely been moved down one hundred and one feet; if they wanted to pay him for another hundred he thought that might clear the line out all the way to the outlet into the harbor, but he couldn't say until he got his contraption into the pipe.

After lunch we convened: Pierre Lambrecht, who is from Belgium, a mechanic in his late forties, a very jovial man with a small military, noncommissioned officer's mustache; Harl, Peter and Mary Tripp's son-in-law, a young Coast Guard officer who specialized in electronics; and myself. Pierre had dug a pit in his garden for the overflow to collect in, rather than run over his entire patch of grass, and now he reckoned we should start digging in Mrs. Silvia's garden, just below the point where his line joined the pipe. Mary Tripp went to call on Mrs. Silvia, and tactfully, in Portuguese, explained the necessity of digging up one of her flower beds. Then we climbed over Peter's fence and down a ladder to the somewhat lower stretch of Silvia garden carrying pitchfork and spade.

Harl did much of the inaugural digging. He was the youngest, a bit of a stranger, and perhaps allusions that Pierre and I made to each other about small babies and paper diapers got to him—in any event, he picked up a pitchfork and went to work, loosening the soil beneath the gladiolae. He dug the earth away until, at a depth of several feet, he reached the rounded, terracotta top surface of the pipe. Here Pierre, who had been advising Harl as to depth and strength of stroke, and suggesting that he take a deep breath between shovel-loads, took over, making a neat hole in the top of the pipe. In the meantime I ran errands and messages. I drove to the small store by the Community Center on the other side of the tracks where Al Lewis, the Borough Warden, or mayor of the village, presided over a grocery counter and also kept, in a back room, the borough "snake"—a one-hundred-foot length of flexible steel. And when I had returned with this, and Pierre had set Harl to work again ramming it along the pipe, I went off again, this time to the hardware store. Pierre was going to need a piece of tin and a two-pound bag of plaster of paris for patching the hole. He reminded me of a sergeant I had known in the army, who was very good at keeping a young, ignorant second lieutenant busy with necessary but distant jobs while the real work was got on with. When I got back with the tin and plaster Pierre asked me to go tell his wife, Mary Tripp, and my wife to fill all the bathtubs, and then, when he shouted the signal, to pull the plugs and flush all the johns.

In fact, this first attempt produced only momentary relief. In the opened pipe a few bubbles appeared, but there was no vortex, no swirling bathwater going suddenly down the unclogged drain. Instead our signal to the three houses caused the noxious tide to rise in our excavation. We stepped hastily to higher ground. Pierre said, "Well, lads, we'd better move further down Mrs. Silvia's garden." Then, working at a point Pierre prescribed after a moment's revery—"I think it was about here, about four feet from the back steps though it was ten years ago, the last time, and they didn't have the concrete driveway then"—Harl and I dug another trench. We had no flowers to move this time, merely a small spruce which Peter later said was well removed, since it had blocked his narrow view of the harbor, to be seen once more down the Silvia driveway. Somewhere

just below the area in which we were now working,
Pierre believed an additional set of sewer lines from
houses on Trumbull Street came to join our line. Since
they weren't backed up, the blockage had to be roughly
at this point. And so it turned out. Another short thrust
with the irksome snake, which tended to flick and whip
and kink, requiring strong hands to hold it; another call
to the three School Street houses ("Okay, flush and pull
the plugs, *now!*"); and then there was a sudden stir in
our muddy cauldron, the slime began to spin, glugging
sounds arose, and Pierre, Harl and I gave each other ten-
tative smiles of success. The sides of the hole reappeared
as the water swiftly drained away. Then the pipe became visible, and the water could be seen rushing down
the pipe. Pierre patched the holes here and in our first
excavation with tin, wrapping the tin and pipe with
bandages of old shirt, soaked in wet plaster. He made
tight, surgeonlike turns with the cloth. The trenches were
next filled in and some of the flowers replaced. Then we
retired back up over the fence to the Lambrechts' garden
and restored the turf in the open pit Pierre had dug to
limit the flood. Doris Lambrecht brought out from her
kitchen three cans of beer, and we raised our cans to
each other in a toast, feeling like old campaigners, glow-
ing with the heat and the comradeship that momentarily
surmounts origin, age, income, and occupation, the result
of spending a long afternoon together in toil on our
common problem.

The next morning the sewer backed up in Mr. Dim-

mock's yard on Trumbull Street. It seemed we had
merely shifted the blockage further down the line, not
quite to the sea. But for a while we had also shifted the
responsibility. A different set of allies gathered to help
Mr. Dimmock, and it was a pleasure to walk down
Trumbull Street and see them digging in his garden. One
could stop for a moment and retail some of the encour-
agement and advice which neighbors (not halting long
enough to get involved) had given us. However, we
were involved again. The Roto-Rooter man was recalled
and ordered to root out the rest of the sewer all the way
to the harbor and to install a clean-out pipe for future
access. The following week an old lady from Trumbull
Street (her age perhaps being considered a diplomatic
feature where the hard-nosed School Street householders
might be concerned) came round with the Roto-Rooter
bill, split nine ways—it worked out at eight dollars and
ninety-eight cents per house.

Right now we are waiting for the main sewers and a
treatment plant that are supposed to be put in. We have
a crisis of sorts every six weeks or so, generally at the
top end of the line in Peter's garden. Peter in fact keeps
an open trench in his yard, next to his lettuce patch, with
an upturned bucket over the hole he has left in his pipe,
ready for the snake to be quickly plunged in.

❧ 13 ❧

"Social pressures" are what those people complain of who suddenly seem to find village life too much for them, and leave for the anonymity of the city, the loneliness of a backcountry farm or a house in the woods. For me, the case would be the reverse. On a farm I would feel the increased pressure of being only with myself. I imagine I would spend a lot of time wondering whether I was completely forgotten—did other people still want to see me? And if I had to go anywhere it would be so much more of a production. I think, moreover, that if I lived in the country surrounded by trees and fields I would be even more jealous of my rights as a proprietor than I am in town, more suspicious of trespassers and hunters, and afraid of developments springing up on adjoining land and superhighways blazing through. There are compensations in living in a place where most of the building has been done that can be done, most of the suspicions aroused that can ever be aroused.

When towns like Stonington were first being settled in Connecticut in the late seventeenth and early eighteenth centuries, men were frowned on if they expressed a desire to move out of the settlement to farmland two or three miles distant. The small town was a religious society, with a meeting house for its center. The struggle to organize a new parish generally succeeded only when the people of one town had shown that they had enough families and wealth to support a minister of their own. In Stonington, the original settlement took place in Wequetequock, at the head of the creek, but the first center for a rather scattered community of planters was further inland, on the Pequot Trail, where the Road Church was established in 1673. Most were farmers, and a few traded with the Indians. Thomas Stanton at Pawcatuck remained a friend of various Indian sachems even after King Philip's War, and on one occasion (one can read in the History of the 1st Congregational Church of Stonington) "Uncas in his old age went from Mohegan to Pawcatuck for Mr. Stanton to write his will, taking with him a train of his noblest warriors to witness the same."

In the course of the next hundred years the center of gravity of Stonington settlement shifted from the Road district to Long Point. It was a site on the water, and water in those days provided the best means of transportation. In 1774 a group of villagers petitioned the General Assembly in Hartford for the right to establish a permanent place of worship in their midst. "The memorial of William Morgan, Benjamin Park, John Denison 4th, Oliver Hillard, Edward Hancox, Oliver

Smith & the rest of the subscribers hereto in behalf of themselves & the professors of the Establish'd Religion of the Colony, living at a place called Long Point in Stonington in the county of New London humbly sheweth . . ." What they testified was that they were four miles from a meeting house; they lived principally by the whale and cod fishery; they were generally poor; their population had increased in recent years to upwards of eighty families—among them, twenty widows, seventeen of whom had children; that they had no more than one horse to every ten families and therefore few could ride four miles to church. The petitioners were broke because they'd had to put their money into building a windmill (they were too far from the grist mill) and also into building a schoolhouse, causeways, and roads (Main Street was laid out in 1752). The fishing was poor at that time, and the markets low. Furthermore, "the various and different sentiments in the religious denomination of Christians among them, viz.: First Day Baptists, Seven Day Baptists, & the Quakers or those call'd Friends, are such real grief and great discouragements to your memorialists, who are of the Establish'd Religion of this Colony, that they can no longer think of obtaining a meeting house by subscription or any other ways among themselves." What they wanted was the right to hold a lottery to raise the money for a meeting house. The permission was given, after a few years; and after a further delay occasioned by the Revolutionary

War, the 2nd Stonington Congregational Church was built. The Minister in 1789 got a hundred pounds a year plus firewood cut and delivered.

Coincident with the movement into the village for practical purposes was the feeling at the time that out in the country lay "disorder and sin." Churches, neighbors, and constables couldn't keep an eye on things. In the mid-eighteenth century Jared Elliot attacked a proposal for new settlement in large, scattered estates. He believed that it was only in towns, where children could attend schools, where "social worship" was available, and where "wild and savage behaviour [was] put out of countenance," that there was "opportunity for the exercise of social virtues." "Outlivers," as the early suburbanites were called, were distinctly further from God. They became a group with their own special interests—in one early Stonington militia election, the people of the town plot formed one party and the outlivers formed another.

Although the religious and social situation is now very changed, and the present village is a much more compact and highly populated community than the "town" was then, there remains in the village a feeling that those who live outside it are different. Those who live out of the village have, to begin with, plumped for one of two contrasting sets of circumstances. They have more room around their houses. They see less of their neighbors. They are more dependent on their telephones and cars.

They tend to be middle and upper income, because zoning demands separate houses of a certain size, and what poor there are seem to be old rural families run to seed living in run-down gray-shingled farmhouses, or new industrial families living in trailer camps.

Many of those who live outside the village may never have lived in it; some may never enter it. They work in New London, perhaps, and shop in Westerly. Although they live in the Town of Stonington, which is what elsewhere in New England would be called a Township, the magnetism of the village center has been diffused by the spread of housing along the country roads. The high school and the new police station are on Route One, halfway to Westerly. The Town Hall is in the Borough (which is the governmental term for the village) but on the wrong side of the tracks; 1930's and red-brick, it doesn't prompt the suggestion of belonging in the village. There was a nine-month period last year when—after Doctor Haliday suddenly died—the village was without a full-time doctor. We seemed to drive a lot then, one way to a professional building situated at an interchange of Federal Interstate highway I-95 (where are located specialists in teeth, children's ailments, and psychiatric disorders), or another way to get an adult checkup or have the record player fixed. I admit to moments of resenting the time-wasting, mobile, multiple-choice-giving suburban society which by its growth, if not by its disorder and sin, threatens to fray the well-bound edges of the village—the place which we live *in*.

On this simple image, however, has to be imposed another—the village is a place not only where people live, or do not live; it is a place where they come and go, and come back again. Some move out when they have teen-age children and move back when their children have married and gone away. Sometimes those who have sold their village houses and moved to a split-level on Flanders Road or an apartment in Pawcatuck feel they would move back if they could afford to (it is significant that the value of property in the village seems to increase faster than that of property outside). One native whom villagers were surprised to see return was John Fish—he had been missing for ten years and was believed dead when he came back from South Africa in 1902, a Captain in the British Army. And some leave and never come back. John and Louis Albertus retired to France in 1885 after being village shoe-makers.* Some of the Portuguese who come and spend thirty or forty years on the fishing draggers or in the velvet-mill retire on social security to the Azores.

But the village allows this. It is not to be located too

---

* Eleanor Perenyi, walking in a mountainside graveyard in Greece, found a headstone marked Eva Palmer, formerly of Stonington, Conn. Miss Palmer had married a Greek poet and helped preserve many notable Greek ruins. Mrs. Perenyi's mobile mother, Mrs. Stone, recalls reading an account of Florentine society in the 1880's—a Miss S—— of Stonington was being acclaimed as the belle of the season.

precisely. Instead of saying it is in the town of Stonington, or in the state of Connecticut, one should perhaps say simply that it is somewhere between New York and the Azores. It allows one to feel for a time that it is a suitable container for one's loyalties—if you belong to it, you don't have to throw in your lot altogether with contemporary America, which is merely a holding company, a conglomerate. Perched on the edge of the continent, and on the edge of the sea, the village gives one the equal possibility of going on or going back—whether, like the Portuguese, to the islands, or like the Yankees (who as they get older become involved in antiques and family trees) into their short and crowded past.

❧ 14 ❧

PARADES FRAME THE SUMMER. The Fourth of July parade is secular, patriotic American, with fire companies, auxiliary policemen, and perky high-school bands. The parade on the first Sunday in September, the day before Labor Day, is religious, patriotic Portuguese, with statues of saints and with little girls in white communion dresses; the band, from Fall River, Massachusetts, plays melancholy Iberian rhythms. Both parades make circuits of the village. People line the sidewalks and stand on the steps of stores or on front porches, while others walk along, adults on the sidewalk, children in the street, keeping pace with the marchers. Marching has become an exceptional activity—the organization of something most people no longer do, which is walk; and because of this it serves better than it ever did for the purposes of celebration or propaganda. A march declares: See, here we are, walking together. It makes more of a point, whether for peace, or unsegregated schools, or simply as here in Stonington to express the pleasure people can take in a tradition and ceremony.

In the village the day before Labor Day is known as

the Holy Ghost—the complete term, Feast of the Holy Ghost, being considered already understood. A similar abbreviation affects the popular account of the actual historic occasion in the sixteenth century of which this is an anniversary celebration: the Holy Ghost, one is told, ended a great famine and fed the masses. A less abridged story would be that Queen Isabella prayed to the Holy Ghost for aid in stopping the rains which were flooding Portugal. Then, when the rains ceased but the crops were ruined, the Queen sold her crown jewels to feed the starving people. And now in Portuguese communities all over the world there are Holy Ghost societies and clubhouses. When Mary Madeira, our babysitter, was asked if she could sit for us that day, she replied that she would be going to the Holy Ghost—and that covered the whole situation, the Holy Ghost parade on the feast of the Holy Ghost commencing and ending at the Holy Ghost club. The club is an asbestos-shingled Greek Revival building on Main Street, next door to the Nathaniel Palmer house, where James McNeill Whistler lived as a child and the family of the poet Stephen Vincent Benét—who wrote "American Names"—lived later on. Portuguese names common in Stonington are De-Bragga, Santos, Costa, Moniz, Faria, Vargas, Silvia, Arruda, Medeiros, Serrano, Narcizzi, Souza, and Mello, among many others. Some names have been easily Americanized to Henry, Lewis, and Roderick. *Festas* and processions have always been the chief holiday amusement of the Portuguese wherever they have lived. In Ponta Delgada in the Azores, the Procession of Santo Christo on the fifth Sunday after Easter was one of the most important, and by the 1920's, when many Portuguese-American emigrants had returned to live on the islands, the procession was accompanied by a fireworks display incorporating the American flag. At the Club on Main Street, the Holy Ghost parade is followed by a fete with sideshows and stalls. There is continuous music and dancing, and a banquet of strong Portuguese soup and ice cream, in celebration of the end of the great famine, free to all comers.

Last year the day dawned gray. Frankie Keane said cheerfully when I went in to pick up the morning paper, "Well, it's the Holy Ghost all right—it'll either rain or snow." It rained all morning. The parade came up School Street in a thick warm drizzle, the Fall River Portuguese brass band playing the slow, sad music that sounds as if it belonged on a faded pianola roll. Rain fogged the glasses of the bandsmen and the transparent plastic slickers which covered their uniforms, gray serge and gold braid. Near the ground, uniformity ceased between gray trouser cuff and wet black shoes; their ankle socks were all colors. Against the weather the top had been raised on the new Ford convertible, driven by the local Ford dealer, which carried Father Loftus, the Reverend Lewis, and the Congregational Minister Mr. Worcester, ecumenically bunched together in the back seat. The rest of the parade did without foul-weather gear. The occasion and the music seemed to be sunny enough for the band of little girls, including two of my own (customarily Protestant) daughters, adorned in frilly white or blue dresses, and the very small child, pale with importance, who carried the crown. She bore it on a white silk cushion, an arrangement of pearls and silver suggesting Isabella's jewels. The American flag was borne on the right, and on the left the Portuguese, carried by my neighbor across the street, Manny Arruda, dressed in his best suit, and soberly smiling at his family as he passed. A tall pastel statue of St. Peter, patron of fishermen, preceded a pick-up truck with a dory in back, and then a car carrying several widows of fishermen.

For most of the year the crown resides in the care of a trusted member of the Holy Ghost society. In the last few weeks before the feast the crown travels from house to house. This year it stayed last across the street at Mrs. Cabral's, placed on a bureau in the front downstairs room where people could see it as they walked past the front door. Surrounded by pink and purple candles, it looked like an exotic birthday cake. Children were beckoned in from the street by Mrs. Cabral to see the crown. Having paid tribute by kissing it, they were given a piece of candy as a souvenir of their visit.

· · ·

❧

IN THE NINETEENTH CENTURY Stonington had many
more Negroes than it does today, with a few well-
integrated black families. In the period when it was a
prosperous railroad town and steamboat port Negroes
worked on the docks and in the hotels. Benjamin Ross,
who was black, ran an ice-cream parlor. William Henry
Wood, a Negro, was a Borough of Stonington bailiff and
constable; in 1891, the oldest member of the force, he
polled the highest vote when he was re-elected to his
post for the sixth consecutive time. In 1880 a black man,
John Francis, who was said to be 108, died in the village.
As a young man he had come from St. Helena, where he
had been a servant of Napoleon. One wonders if he sat
in Benjamin Ross's ice-cream parlor and related his
memories. Hank Palmer (who is now in his early fifties)
remembers the African Baptist church, which used to
stand next door to his father's house on Water Street. It
had a congregation of a hundred and fifty or so in the
steamboat era, but was down to a score of enthusiasts by
the time he was a child. When it was finally put up for
sale and someone planned to turn it into a dance hall,
Mr. Palmer, Sr., bought it for the then very high price of
seven thousand dollars. Eventually the old church build-

ing was moved across the tracks and when it burned out a few years ago was in use as the headquarters of the Daughters of Isabella, Nina Circle.

I mention the Negro past for several interrelated reasons. For one thing, it was a period that many older people miss. Joe Costa, now in his late seventies, came here at the age of ten with his parents from the islands. He says, "This was a lively place then. It's half dead now." What was the basis of the liveliness? Joe sucks on his pipe and thinks. "Ah, it was the trains." When the village was a center of public transportation it was lively. There were trains, steamers, strangers, hotels, and turnover. A second reason is that many of the Portuguese are somewhat tetchy about the fact that some of them have African blood. The Portuguese in their colonies have always been good mixers, with no great prejudice about intermarriage. On the mainland they mixed with the Moors and on many of the islands, particularly the Cape Verdes, with Negroes. The man who lived in the upstairs apartment at 16 School Street before we bought it was quite black. There is one small boy who delivers newspapers, whose nickname is Cinnamon—he is in fact a very sunny, cheerful color. What on the wider village scale this touch of color does, however, is tinge the antagonism which occasionally flares up between those villagers who are in general descendants of Northern Europeans and those villagers who are generally Iberian. It makes for a certain amount of racial tension. It makes it easier for sides to be taken and lines to be drawn. "Them uptown" is one way the Portuguese have of describing the Yankees on Main Street—carrying the implication that all Yankees live on Main Street and are rich stuffed shirts. The Yankees fire back with "Black Portugees!" There is no doubt that some Portuguese deserve being put into such categories as emotional, fatalistic, impulsive, vindictive, and mean to their hard-working women. There is equally little doubt that some Yankees are inbred and addle-brained. "Swamp Yankee" used to be a term bearing connotations of native wit and resourcefulness; but now it seems better connected with a red-necked obstinacy, a sort of frontier suspicion that regards all men as enemies until they've shown signs of being otherwise—and sometimes not even then.

Time, of course, erases differences. Portuguese bread is now an elite delicatessen item, replaced by Wonderbread and Mr. Big in the diets of Portuguese families. The language is slowly fading from use, despite new arrivals from the islands; the first generation hangs on to it when talking to each other and the elderly; the second generation makes fun of it; and the third generation, going to college, may study and teach it. For that matter, although some old Portuguese return to Fayal or São Miguel after a working lifetime here, others remain. Their bones lie in St. Mary's Cemetery at the head of Lamberts Cove. The land for this burial ground was given to the church by Frank Silvia, who came from the Azores in the 1840's and prospered in real estate, the ice

business, and construction work. In 1893 (according to
Don Lewis, himself a descendant of Portuguese settlers)
Frank Silvia and his sons had the job of tearing down the
old Wadawanuck Hotel, which the railroad had built on
the site of the present library. With the lumber they built
several village houses and repaired many others. A few
decades earlier Frank Silvia had helped build the former
St. Mary's Church on Wadawanuck Square. It stood
until five years ago, a simple, not very elegant, white-
painted clapboard structure. Perhaps its simple virtues
were less evident to those not of the faith. At any rate,
it became too small for the growing flock and has been
replaced by a big white-brick church, whose sprawling
barnlike nave is both out of scale and out of keeping
with the replica of an early New England Congregational spire that is perched on top. If the Gothic
cathedrals expressed medieval man's soaring aspirations
to worship God, this new St. Mary's (as several members of the congregation pointed out to the building
committee in the planning stage) seems to express the
worldly desire of its parishioners to show that they've
made it here on earth—at least as much as the Congrega-
tionalists and Baptists, united down the street, or the
Episcopalians in their imitation Victorian-Norman-
Saxon 1849 stone chapel a few blocks away. St. Mary's
has an extensive parking lot. But even that can't contain
the cars that drive in from all over the surrounding
countryside to the Masses on Sunday mornings.

The Portuguese-Yankee split is abetted by a touch of

race and a strong dollop of religious difference, but most
of the time it remains latent. Several things help here.
For one thing, the Portuguese inferiority complex is alle-
viated by political success—it is easier for a Portuguese
to get elected to Borough office than for someone
stamped as a Yankee. (Hank Palmer was born in the village, has spent most of his life here, founded the boat
works, and headed the library board and the school
board, but when he ran for the post of Borough Warden,
he failed to win by a fair margin. One lady of Portuguese descent told me flatly she would never vote for a
member of the Wadawanuck Club—and Hank Palmer
had been president of that, too.) Moreover, a sufficient
number of people seem to share the Portuguese suspicion
of the Yankees as a breed with too strong an attachment
to the past—to old houses, old trees, old atmospheres,
even old stocks and bonds—all of which may militate
against present opportunities to make a living. The present president of the Historical Society threw a scare into
many people a few years ago when he proposed a Historical District. This apparently would have controlled
the kind of alterations made to land and buildings within
the district. But what, in that case, about aluminum
storm windows? How about television aerials? Not to
mention small workshops, stores, industries, commercial
traffic and cars—would it be all right and not anachro-
nistic to park, say, a 1970 Chevrolet station wagon outside
a historic 1776 house? As it is, the Yankees are always

planting trees wherever they can, and it is the Portuguese of the Borough street cleaning crew who have to sweep up all the leaves.

Stonington is the only port in Connecticut that feels the effect of the open sea. It faces a gap left by Fishers Island and the eastern tips of Long Island, through which the Atlantic rolls in from the southeast until it breaks on the chain of reefs running from Wicopesset to Napatree. For several hundred years the village has made a good part of its living from the sea. In the memorial addressed to the Hartford General Assembly in 1774 the Congregational petitioners said they lived principally by the whale and cod fishery. Two hundred whales were reported in Fishers Island Sound in October 1799. Sealing and whaling in distant waters brought prosperity to the town and fortunes to individuals in the first half of the nineteenth century. It was the age of captains who made great voyages, Cutlers, Fannings, and Palmers. While in command of a small sloop, the *Hero*, Nathaniel Palmer discovered the Antarctic Continent. In mid-century, when the Yankees were no longer as keen to embark on voyages that might last three years, it was sealing and whaling ships, stopping for crews in the Azores and Cape Verdes, which brought the first Portuguese to Stonington. Here many of them went on fishing inshore, handlining for cod and haddock from small sailing boats that were docked on the east side of the Point. In this century the boats got bigger; large steam-engined bunker boats collected fish from barrel traps and shore seines along the Rhode Island beaches. In the twenties and thirties the diesel-engined fifty- and sixty-foot draggers were introduced that are still in use today— boats named *Luann, Marise, Fairweather, Dauntless,* and *America*—some of them rather worn, some rigorously maintained. The work produced tough, independent men—their own bosses, not paid by the hour, who became constitutionally and temperamentally unable to work in a factory, not that any of them would actually admit to such a thing as "loving" the sea. One family, the Rodericks, came from Terceira in the Azores in 1907. The father, Manuel Roderick, Sr., had fourteen children, eight of them boys who followed him to sea. The old man, despite the loss of both legs, kept fishing until his death. He sat in the pilot house of his dragger, strapped to a chair behind the wheel. On his final trip in 1945 the *Alice & Jenny* went on the rocks off Block Island. Captain Roderick was cut loose by his men, and his son George carried him piggy-back to safety through the surf.

The fortunes of the fishing fleet declined after World War II. Some Stonington boats went off to other ports such as Point Judith and New Bedford. The fishermen complained about the village: the lack of good docks, trucking facilities, filet plants or fish-rendering factories. Critics of the fishermen said that they had poor boats, obsolete equipment, and outmoded ideas—they were bad husbandmen of their resources, and often completely fished-out an area and then wondered why succeeding years brought smaller harvests. In 1961, when we came to the village, the fleet was down to fewer than ten boats. It moored at the decrepit wooden piers behind Bindloss's hardware store and oil depot, and at the former railroad terminal and steamboat dock, then called Longo's after its owner—a dusty, bumpy wilderness with a few old storage shacks, rough stone embankments, and rotten fenders and pilings to which the draggers tied up.

In the mid-sixties the situation came to a head. Anthony Longo offered to sell his dock and adjoining land to the town for $350,000. A town meeting was called to decide whether or not to buy it. At that point the town had a good reason to buy it, since it was being compelled (like other towns) by the federal government to clean up its polluted waters and install a sewage system. Longo's and the adjacent land would make an excellent site for a treatment plant. If the town bought the site for those purposes, it could fix up the dock along the way as a proper base of operations for the Stonington fishing boats.

The issue was immediately bedeviled with red herrings. In the Yankee camp, the anxiety was *smell*, not so much from a sewage plant but from the fish-rendering plant which—it was suggested—would be built if the town owned the dock. Wouldn't it be better to use the site for some attractive private houses? On the other

side, supporters of the fishermen went round yelling that
the Yankees wanted to buy up all the remaining waterfront and turn it to their selfish ends. It was true that a
fish-rendering plant might produce dreadful odors. It
was true that the number of places where the ordinary
citizen could reach the water in the village were fast declining behind private fences. However, both wings
tended to ignore economics, planning opinion, sanitation
engineering advice, and indeed any reasoned, balanced
argument. If you were heard to say that, well, there
might be a better place for a sewage treatment plant
though it seemed no one was looking very hard, then
you were at once accused of being anti-fisherman, anti-
Portuguese, and a stuffed shirt. If you opined (to the
stuffed shirts) that you thought the town ought to do
something for the fishermen in spite of their obsolete
ways because fish was one real reason the place had
character and wasn't just a cute New England beauty
spot, then you were taken as a damned advocate of fish
flour, fish factories, and the consequent acrid stink which
would envelop the whole community. (There were similar controversies in New England villages at the beginning of the nineteenth century over whether or not to
install stoves in churches. The member of one church
said of his minister, "If Mr. Merrill needs a fire, let him
go to the Other Place where they keep one year round."
In 1831 a stove was installed in the basement of the
meeting house at Southington, Connecticut, and services

were held there for seven years while the congregation
made up its mind whether it was right and proper to install one upstairs.)

The town meeting to decide the Longo's Dock business was held in the senior high school on the road to
Westerly. Since it was a town and not just a village
matter, the auditorium was crowded. There was a section of outlivers' opinion that seemed to feel the town
was spending a lot of money for the sake of the village:
what good did the fishermen or a sewer system do the
rest of the population? However, scattered in Pawcatuck, East Mystic, and the backroad developments there
lived fishermen and the many relations of fishermen.
They spread the word that decent docking facilities
were what they really needed, and they assured voters
that if the town provided them, the fishermen's association would be a good tenant of the dock. At the town
meeting, the First Selectman and other proponents of the
scheme claimed that there would be room on the site for
the fishermen, a treatment plant, and some landscaped
recreation space. Opponents complained about the cost.
Some people made short, pithy speeches and others made
long ones full of hard-to-follow argument and scarcely
relevant detail. There were cheers and shouts and hot
tempers. Clearly you had to be on one side or the other.
When John Dodson, Sr., the operator of the boat yard
and employer of many Portuguese, stood up in order to
get some light thrown on one aspect of the plan, namely

that the dock might be a municipally sponsored competitor for him, providing public wharfage for yachts as well as fishing boats, the uproar was immense. By that time the will of the majority was obviously in favor of the town purchasing the dock. Among the yells and catcalls drowning out John Dodson's question could be heard the voice of Mrs. Rita, the Dodsons' cleaning lady, screaming, "Sit down, you old bastard!" Of course next day she was back at work, feeding the Dodson dogs and dusting the downstairs.

A few years after this, it's possible to say that already the property looks like a good investment. There is no fish factory. A couple of draggers have joined the fleet, and many more lobster boats; lobstering is booming. The dock has been greatly improved with new pilings and concrete reinforcements of the dock walls. The whole area has been leveled and graded, so that trucks can drive up to the loading wharf with no fear of breaking an axle, and on several grassed stretches children can chase around and fly kites. The treatment plant is about to be built in an unprominent position. At Dodson's Boat Yard, summer brings as much business as the yard can handle. The only problems Dodson's has had in the recent past have been the result of some Yankee private investors purchasing the abandoned railroad property, between Longo's dock and the boat yard, causing Dodson's to worry about having to move several piers.

For that matter, on the evening of the Holy Ghost,

when a block party is going on with a Portuguese core but much of the village participating, the front door of the Dodsons' house nearby is always invitingly open, and quite often the overflow from the street party goes in.

⇜ 15 ⇝

FALL RETURNS US TO OURSELVES, the essential villagers. Summer distractions have gone. We can resume old companionships, get back to more diligent work, and take up veteran animosities. Where summer expands the village population and brings in many new faces, allowing a novel and much wider choice of acquaintances and a greater possibility of like to talk to like, autumn constricts our circle again; the rich and the poor, the hearty and the intellectual once more have to put up with each other as well as they can—which sometimes isn't very well at all. Next-door neighbors who have had different things to do and different people to see since Memorial Day now re-realize each other's existence. Women who for the past two months have managed to unload their children on summer friends (who were, at least to begin with, glad to have knowledgable local kids for their city-deprived youngsters to play with), now find their children, and all the children from nearby houses, continually in and out. There are wars, from which the defeated go bawling home. On front steps and porches mothers are heard defending their progeny against the loud accusations of other mothers. Income, accent, occupation, and education exaggerate all other natural differences. Doors slam.

On School Street the spark of a dispute often arises from parking problems. On this street and others in what the Borough Warden and Burgesses sometimes refer to as "the congested Point section," two- and even three-family houses are prevalent. Many of the families in these houses have children in their late teens whose earliest and soonest realized ambition is to own a car, preferably a large Chevrolet or Pontiac convertible, with chromed tailpipes and hubcaps modeled after those on Etruscan war chariots. It is a rare thing for the man of a family not to own a car, but even if he doesn't, his wife is probably earning enough at the mill or cleaning "uptown" houses to afford one of her own—first taking an instruction course with Mr. Marino, whose ulcer the whole village has a share in. If they fail the test, they usually have a daughter graduating from high school into hairdressing or secretarial work and willing to assume the responsibility for the 385-horsepower GT SST that has already been bought, or down-paymented. So some three-family houses are responsible for six or seven cars. Given the state of public transportation, in part cause but mostly the effect of this, it is vacuous to complain about them. (At the turn of the century there was an excellent trolley service between Westerly and Groton. Bus service is now reduced to a paltry one a day. In fact, we have reached such a zenith of laissez-faire or a nadir of public service that there is not even a taxicab in the village. One has to be summoned from Westerly or Mystic.)

Parking complications increase because of the narrow streets, which permit parking on one side only. Then there are driveways to private garages, say one for every third or fourth house, and the driveways remove curb space at least equal to the car in the garage. (Sometimes in the evenings when he comes in from driving around the block looking for a parking space, Peter Tripp will take to his drawing board and produce exotic schemes for ridding the streets of parked vehicles; one I especially liked was a sort of davit which swung out over the sidewalk and lifted the car, lifeboat-fashion, up over the front porch.) There are further problems. Parking is a point on which contact is first made between the fenders of cars, and then between the even more fragile temperaments of their owners. Here, as with the geese and rats the Austrian ethologist Konrad Lorenz has studied, "excessive propinquity causes excessive adrenal flow and other glandular changes. [I quote Joseph Alsop's review in *The New Yorker* of Lorenz's work.] Even in species whose inhibitions are iron-strong, aggression becomes intra-specific; the members of the overcrowded population spring upon one another."

Most of the time on School Street we don't feel overcrowded and particularly on top of one another; but we do occasionally feel the excessive propinquity of Henry Wilson, a fisherman. For four or five days at a time Wilson is out on his boat, and the only evidence of him is his Buick sedan parked outside the Wilson house, whose ground-floor apartment is rented to a carless elderly couple, both deaf. But then for another three or four days Wilson is home. Out of the workshop behind his house come forth his home-made camping trailer, a racing stock car, and other assorted wheeled vehicles he has in various stages of construction and which—while working on one or another of them in his driveway—he leaves in parking spots vacated by other residents of the street, who have gone off to work or to shop. Coming back from the supermarket with a full load of groceries or arriving home in the early dawn from the Electric Boat night shift, they find Wilson's armada in all the spaces. Even when he is off fishing, and his unused Buick could be parked in his driveway, Wilson leaves it parked in front of his house, occupying a space—in fact, such is the man's nature, parked at a half-car length from the entrance to his drive and thus occupying a space and a half.

Everyone on the street at one time or other gets upset about Wilson, and the most aggrieved are those who live closest to him. (The one person on the street who is friendly with him lives two houses away, reminding one of the Franco-Russian entente, possible because Germany and Poland were in between.) The lady who lives on one side once tried to outwit Wilson. She waited in her car someway up the street until Henry Wilson fired up his Buick and moved it down to a vacant spot outside the Pasquales' preparatory to bringing out part of his wheeled inventory. Then she buzzed into the Buick's former slot with her modest Volkswagen and left it there for two days. Retribution was not slow in coming. Wilson waited until it was parked elsewhere and then boxed it in with his Buick and his stock car. Since he then went fishing, the men of the street had to lift the VW out sideways.

When the Coogans lived on the street, they had some friends one night who left their car parked briefly in the entrance to Wilson's driveway. In a moment he appeared, revved up the Buick, backed up and braked hard within an inch of the visitor's front fender, blew his horn, and eventually came and knocked on the Coogans' door and demanded that they move the vehicle. The Coogans waited a few nights before returning the favor. We had gone out, but heard about it from a young couple named the Higleys. They had been told of a house for rent on School Street; since it was a fine October night, they walked down to have a peek at it. However, as they came round the corner of Omega Street, a police car backed wildly up the hill and stopped athwart the entrance to School Street, red light flashing, blocking incoming traffic. The policeman, talking to headquarters on his radio, was saying something about riot precautions. Going on down School Street, the Higleys saw a small crowd gathered outside Wilson's house. They were shouting, "Come on out and fight, Henry Wilson, come on out and fight." The Coogans had given a party for some out-of-town friends, and on their way home the friends decided to repay the hospitality by working off the Coogans' grudge for them. But Wilson did not appear. In a minute or two, when the shouting had slackened, the policeman walked down the street and tactfully suggested that "all you folks ought to be getting along now." They got along. The Higleys rented elsewhere.

Yet Wilson was less bothersome for a month or so after this. Like the male stickleback, as observed by the Dutch scientist Niko Tinbergen, Wilson's lonely energies spill over into what Tinbergen calls "displacement activity"—instead of fighting, the stickleback goes through elaborate defensive ceremonies on the borders of his territory, digging nests in the sand with jerking and thrusting movements: "it is as if the animal is hitting an opponent, but the peculiar thing is that it is not aimed at the opponent itself but at the bottom, which is the object of the sand-digging." Wilson at these times works on the fence around his yard, hammering new boards onto uprights and coating them with thick white paint. He puts a new roof on his garage and replaces the screens in his storm windows.

· · ·

❧

IN FALL I SOMETIMES WORK on the inside of my own cas-
tle. In the course of eight years of living in it, the house
has been "improved"—several closets have been built,
and a few walls of crumbling horsehair plaster replaced
(and the opportunity taken to install fiberglass insulation
behind the new sheet-rock). One fall I replaced the
treads on the stairs, some of which were rotten, and another autumn I built myself a study in the attic. Not all
the improvements have been utilitarian. The children
think the best thing in the house is the swing we built in
the living room—a piece of seven-inch pine shelving
saved from the kitchen of our last New York apartment,
on West 75th Street, now suspended on two Dacron
bridles from lengths of blue polypropylene lobster-pot
warp. These pieces of line are spliced to two snap hooks,
and the hooks hook onto big galvanized screw eyes
screwed into the fir beam that runs across the room,
holding up the ceiling and the bathtub. People who come
into the room for the first time invariably make for the
swing, and swing on it. Little girls swing and make up
songs on it. Boys pump it higher and higher until they
can touch the ceiling, and leave the marks of their shoes
and even knees on the ceiling. Pretty women swing and

look even prettier. It keeps babysitters amused better than television, and only once in a while does a child fall off, generally because he's been showing off vaingloriously. It teaches lessons and often soothes bad tempers. My children have had the chance to become acrobatic aces on it. Elderly admirals sit on the swing and float cautiously with their shoes skimming the floor, like the pontoons of a seaplane ready for an emergency landing.

These projects generally take me down to the lumberyard, where the Perrys, father and son, are full of good carpentry advice and Paul Moody will stop for a moment from mixing paint or cutting glass to discuss sundials; he is a sundial enthusiast. And in other places on fall afternoons one can drop in to feel the village pulse: the library, Mr. Siegel's department store, or Squadrito's, which is one of the three barber shops, and the one I prefer. It isn't just the quality of the cut, or the vacuum cleaner which Mr. Squadrito uses to remove the loose hair from under one's collar. The superiority of Squadrito's resides in the fact that there are always people there, talking. Social historians say that barber shops are not what they were; that there was a golden age before the invention of the safety razor, when numbered shaving mugs could be rented from the barber if you didn't keep your own named mug there, and when the presence of the *Police Gazette*, the *Playboy* of yesteryear, made a wait for a shave or a haircut worthwhile. But at Squadrito's conversation is still lively. The men discuss whether the Hartleys are going on a world cruise again this year, what the Plymouth dealer thinks of this year's Plymouth, how much Al Davis paid for his initialed license plates, how many more school buses are being leased this semester, and whether old Robinson is really going to sell his ice house this time; if he does, where's he going to put his collection of five hundred major league baseball bats? At Squadrito's it often turns out that half the people aren't waiting for a haircut—they just came in to chat. And others pop in from time to time for quick visits. The on-duty policeman reads a few pages of *Popular Mechanics.* The linen-supply man brings clean towels and smocks. Several local businessmen bring or take away a dollar or two (I've never found out whether for chamber of commerce dues, horses, or insurance payments). Mr. Siegel pops in, returning the barber shop copy of the New York *Daily News.*

In the Book Mart on Wadawanuck Square the gossip has a slightly different tone. At this equinoctial time people who have lived in the village for any length watch the sky and sniff the air, and can be seen gazing at the tops of the trees on Main Street—the replacements and survivors of the great elms decimated by the hurricane of 1938. "It feels like a hurricane to me," says elderly Miss Stimson, a former college dean and professor of history, encountered in the Book Mart. John Dodge, a retired architect, says the weather reminds him of that which preceded an earthquake he once went through in

Turkey. In fact, there have been earth tremors in this part of New England—October 29, 1727, for one, and also on April 1, 1828. In Stonington windows broke, doors threw themselves open, great noises were heard, and for several days there was a heavy swell at sea. The 1938 hurricane brought huge waves which swept away forty houses on Napatree, sank most of the fishing boats and yachts in the harbor, and demolished houses on Hancox Street and Wall Street, then still called Shinbone Alley—it was where many of the Negroes used to live. Three people were drowned in Shinbone Alley. The old trees came down, and the New Haven shoreline express was stranded halfway across the embankment spanning the upper harbor. Many people in the village remember this storm—it impressed them, deeply enough to last a lifetime, with a knowledge of what nature could do when it got properly tuned up; hearing of hurricanes, they think immediately of storm shutters and higher ground.

One person who vividly remembers September 21, 1938, is Mrs. Evelyn Cole, a very spry little lady who is to be seen swimming at the Club in the late summer evenings, when the swimming float is less crowded, or driving her laundry down to Mrs. Narcizzi on School Street, the top of her wide-brimmed hat barely visible over the steering wheel of her car. Mrs. Cole, now seventy-nine and a widow, was a whiz at the real-estate business, and her ads in *The New York Times*—"charming house in

historic New England seaport village"—brought many
city people to Stonington. "Oh we had a time that day,"
says Mrs. Cole. "The Curtises were moving into our
house, Ragged Edge, at the foot of Omega Street—nice
people, we'd let them have it for not too much money.
Mrs. Curtis said they weren't good tenants, and we
should take out the stuff that we cared for. So Walter
and I spent the morning doing that. We were living in
the cottage next door, the Barnacle, right on the water's
edge—no, it's not there now. We had a few houses
which we'd done up, put our furniture in to make them
look nice, and then rented. Walter had suffered on the
stock market and we needed whatever we got. Anyway,
when we first heard about the storm we went down into
the cellar of the Barnacle. When anything dreadful is
about to happen I feel the need to be close to stone. We
had a colored couple with us. The man's name was Malcolm. Malcolm said he thought it was a hurricane. It
smelled like one. He'd been in one down south. I said,
don't be silly, but through the cellar windows we could
see those big yellow waves getting higher and higher.
Pretty soon we thought we'd better get out. The whole
house was jumping and shaking, but Walter went upstairs and put on a tie. He felt he'd better be properly
dressed if it were a hurricane. He also put a bottle of
whiskey in his coat pocket. I made sure I was wearing
my pearls. Then we crawled up Omega Street to the
top of the hill. By then the wind was making the sort of
noise you hear in a sawmill, a fierce screaming whine.

We went into one of the Portuguese houses on the hill. They gave me some high-heeled slippers that were too tight, but I put them on. I guess we were wet through. Walter brought out the whiskey and we all had some. Malcolm said he needed some bad, he was getting a cold, and colored folks' colds were worse than white folks' colds. So Walter gave him an extra strong dose. Then we heard the Barnacle go. There was a loud bang as it floated off its foundations and blew against the house Pat Willson has now—you know, she found my silver shoe-horn when they were digging foundations for her new garage. Well, we went upstairs, I forget why, perhaps they thought we needed a place to be by ourselves. The house was shaking, shaking. We opened a door, a bed-room, with a big walnut bed, and there in the middle of it was this dark-skinned couple going at it. I remember the man had tight black hair, and the woman who was underneath him yelled at us, 'Get out! Get out!' I think that's something, don't you? At the height of the hurri-cane."

Walter and Evie Cole borrowed two thousand dol-lars from an uncle, and that got them through the next few months. Walter hired a crew of carpenters and set about repairing houses. The Borough Warden and Bur-gesses put the Coles in charge of a tree-planting cam-paign to replace the elms that had been smashed by the hurricane; the dogwood trees in Wadawanuck Square and the trees on Main Street, now thirty years old, were planted at that time.

⚒ 16 ⚒

I NEGLECTED TO MENTION one occasion when you can
find parking space outside Henry Wilson's house, and
that's Halloween. Not one to risk a broken antenna or
candle wax on his car windows, Wilson takes his Buick
off the street the day before and doesn't put it back until
the day after. I can't say that I'm fond of the occasion
myself. As adults, a certain trepidation enters our
thinking about Halloween for precisely the reason the
prospect excited us as children—mischief. And as adults,
our imaginations encompass a far more extensive range
of pranks—and pranks running over into hooliganism—
than we ever dared get up to as children. The rashest
Halloween act I participated in as a teenager was
throwing eggs at a police car in Davenport, Iowa. To
most children now the night means vast quantities of
candy, with the phrase "trick or treat" reduced to a ritu-
alized password that brings forth without fail wide-open
goody bags. The situation is perhaps encouraged by
adults scared of the one child in a hundred who—bidden
to trick rather than be treated—scrawls abuse on the
fence; and in the village, a few may remember the Att-

water boys who one night (it didn't have to be Halloween for them) piled a Main Street porch high with newspapers and old leaves, and then set fire to it. (A variation
to this trick, which seems to have a tradition behind it, is
to pile the leaves and paper on top of a heap of horse dirt
or cow dung. Thus, in stamping out the flames, the en-
raged householder generally goes in shin-deep.)

As things are, vandalism in the village on Halloween
has been limited by a fancy-dress parade. Led by the
largest fire truck, with red lights flashing, the parade
makes a circuit of the village, ending at the fire-house,
where prizes are awarded to the best goblin, witch, and
monster, and to such seasonal or contemporary costume
entries as corncobs and rocket ships. Ice cream and soda
are served. After the children are sent home, the police
feel justified in kicking any late prowlers off the streets.
The parade also restores to Halloween some of its lost
spookiness; although some adults chicken out, shut up
their houses, and go to the city for the night, many get
into the weird spirit of the occasion. After all, it was
once All Hallows Eve. It now provides a chance to dress
up and wear a mask. One man takes a great deal of de-
light in wearing a convincing plastic likeness of Barry
Goldwater and wandering round the village streets,
thumping on the back some of the more earnest
Republicans he encounters, and telling them to keep up
the good work. Often they can't quite recall where
they've seen that face before. It's a bit upsetting. The op-

portunity for a little out-of-doors transvestism is jumped at by a few: one man dressed in a frilly net creation looked like the fairy queen in an old-fashioned English pantomime. Another person wearing a black suit, black bow tie, and top hat, with an all too real suggestion of expertise as an undertaker—a figure of death out of an Ingmar Bergman film—turned out to be on a close look into the eyes (which seen in a dim street were full of a curious, crazy light) the sweet and contemplative wife of someone we knew; we thought we knew them pretty well. My friend Johnny Dodson Junior used to enjoy climbing into a hunchback costume, pulling on a rubber mask that had fangs, green eyes, and the proper Dracula-like slathering awfulness, and have his wife, Tricia, pour a bottle of tomato ketchup over him. Then, hauled along by his four-year-old son at the end of a chain—the boy wearing a white suit and looking like a dwarf attendant from a mental hospital—Johnny the monster loped along the streets, knocking on doors and trick or treating some of the stuffier families. He jumped out from behind trees on rambling youngsters, a number of whom took to their heels at the nightmarish sight. Small children began to whimper that they wanted to go home now and grown-ups apprehensively crossed to the far side of the street.

．　．　．

In the Village

◄§§►

THE ATTWATERS were a year-round Halloween. They are scattered now, and the boys are grown, but several years ago half a dozen of them lived with their mother in a two-family house not far from us. The neighbors complained of singing and dancing at all hours, and parties of sailors staggering out late at night. Although most of the families close at hand got on with Mrs. Attwater by screaming at her, Mavis Dollart up on School Street used to go with her to the Thursday-night bingo at St. Mary's. Mr. Attwater, a fisherman, was said to be living in Fall River, Mass. He had formerly kept his dragger at Point Judith, closer to Stonington and to Mrs. Attwater. But one day, hearing that her husband was keeping another woman at Point Jude, the good lady drove up there with the intention of taking her half of their joint property. She got to the dragger, took up a fire axe, and started the separation process, beginning on the radar set. In court she received a suspended sentence—the children were a factor in keeping her out of jail, either because the judge thought they needed her care or because he decided they were already punishment enough. Henry Chapin knew them in their prime, and still talks passionately of them. They would swing past his house in the mornings on the way to school and whip off the heads of all the flowers in his front flower bed. The lady opposite once came out to admonish them for writing on his fence and was astonished to find them oral as well as literate. She said, "I'm a naval officer's wife, but some of the words they used were new to me." Henry also ascribed the loss of a rowing boat to the Attwaters. He thought it was the craft used by an Attwater-led youthful gang that rowed through the moorings one night and gathered a fine haul: stopwatches, binoculars, compasses, radios, sleeping bags. Two of the older boys were once caught putting the youngest in the dryer at the laundromat. Lamps broken in Wadawanuck Square or four-letter words incised on the Gothic masonry of Calvary Church were, justly or unjustly, credited to their account.

Yet, although they were scourges on Main Street and "uptown," the Attwater boys always seemed well enough behaved on Hancox, School, and Omega streets. It was home territory; and apart from affection, they probably suspected that if they pulled something there on their own turf, it wouldn't be a matter of the cops being called and their ma getting bawled out for letting them loose—rather it would be a matter of informal, local justice, with the older and tougher youths beating them up. Furthermore, as Henry Chapin discovered long before any of his fellow Main Streeters, the Attwaters were "all right" if you got them on your side, which often meant just giving them a money-earning job to do. Cutting grass, they lost interest in decimating flowers. I got one of them, Ted, to help clean the old coal hole in my cellar, and later he and a brother helped me lift lead ballast out of a boat. I paid them fifty cents apiece and had nothing but politeness and friendliness thereafter.

In the end they moved to Groton, and though some of the boys make return trips, staying with an aunt and hanging out with old pals, the village is no longer hyperconscious of them. On their street Mrs. Attwater fired a parting shot in the form of a large, crudely lettered sign: FOR SALE! BIG FAMILY HOUSE. COLORED PREFERRED. However, the house was eventually sold to a Portuguese-descended family, white, with four little boys.

❦

I SOMETIMES THINK as I walk along a village street at night that it might be a good thing to have a slightly less developed sense of propriety or respect for property— whichever it is that prevents me from walking, not in the street but in some absent householder's garden or yard, and there having a look around. My wife is embarrassing to walk with, since she has very little of this inhibitory sense, and will take rapid advantage of a dark night and an unlocked gate. But she was brought up by her father with the poaching urge. When no rabbits were to be caught on their walk across a farmer's fields, they used to catch some cabbages, and carry them home under their raincoats. She has the feeling still that no one should come back from a walk empty-handed.

In October I walk home with a few pieces of driftwood, found among the rocks at the foot of Wall Street or washed onto the little landing place by the Wad Club tennis courts; fuel for the Franklin stove which will burn on winter nights. Taking a drive on the back roads we pick up logs, pruned from trees by telephone men and lying by the ditches. There are other preparations to be made for winter—summer screens to be removed and put away after the last chance of one of those sultry days in late October. Putting in storm windows presents an opportunity to wash windows, to weatherstrip with caulking putty joints that don't fit very well, and to tack battens over a sheet of polyvinyl which covers the screen door into the garden. Seen through this material, the garden no longer presents clear, edged shapes, but becomes hazy and impressionistic—almost as if a summer fog were tethered there for the winter and had the sharp winter sun shining through it. In parts of Maine and New Hampshire, farmers still pile hay around the foundations of their houses to keep out the ground-whistling winds. Here we go down to the lumberyard and collect several large free boxes of sawdust and shavings to cover the bulbs and otherwise wait for a thick early snowfall to insulate the foundations. Into the cellar go rakes, spades, the garden hose, coiled right-handed and tied in several places so it won't be a kinky mess in spring, and then the weighty, ancient lawnmower, acquired from the Thrift Shop. I drop oil into all its ascertainable orifices and give the rusty blades a last backward spin. Putting all this gear into the cellar involves cleaning out the cellar, and that involves a trip to the dump. After that the side yard needs sweeping. By the time the front porch has been cleared up, it looks as if it could do with a coat of paint.

I like these months of autumn and, when the last leaves have been swept away by an end-of-November gale and the Borough highway crew, I enjoy Thanksgiving, though we no longer bring in a harvest and perhaps give thanks too soon—the feast might be more appropriate at the end, rather than at the beginning, of winter. But for a month or so there seem to be plenty of benevolence and good cheer. The first thick snow falls in big, sticky flakes, and wielding shovels we encounter each other in boots and galoshes, loudly commiserating with one another when the Borough plow turns back the snow from the street onto the sidewalks we have just cleared. Across the street Mrs. Arruda, wielding a lusty shovel, says, "Yeah, some of them uptown don't even bother to clear their sidewalks." Some of *them* are summer residents who have forgotten to arrange to have their sidewalks cleared by local youngsters, and some are year-round natives who neglect the task from indolence or spite.

Snow brings us out into the streets together, but there are other occasions that gather the village. At the Town Fair in August, parents of all backgrounds barge forward democratically as they push their children on board the hay-wagon, or attempt to buy balloons before the balloon man sells out, or to grab the best books on the bookstall. Queues, orderly lines, are not well known here; there has never been a dire shortage of anything that would give rise to such organization. The funeral of Doctor Haliday (after his sudden death) brought together many of us who had in common the fact that we were his patients, had been given by him shots and inspections, had our children delivered by him and all our ailments and pretended ailments ministered to. We all liked him, or respected his crusty humor. We felt jointly bereaved—and we also felt the sudden lack of a village practitioner.

The death of John Kennedy was a disaster of different scale. It was huge—it was felt in cities, towns, and villages everywhere—and it was also personal; it seemed to strike at everyone separately, individually. There was nothing binding about it. Everyone stayed in his own home, watching the television screen, wet-eyed, tight-

chested. I couldn't stand it. I walked around the village
—it was a gray November afternoon, and the vacancy
of the place was for a moment immense. I was on my
own. We were all on our own.

Spontaneous assemblies take place when there are
fires. "The houses being wood, none were seen to fall,"
Hardy reported apologetically to his superiors after
bombarding the village. But the militia had been kept
busy extinguishing the fires started by the Congreve
rockets. (British Navy Congreve rockets successfully
burned down neutral Copenhagen in 1807.) We need
little reminding that we live in a wooden town. The premium of my house insurance policy is partly based on
the distance from the nearest fire hydrant (though it
doesn't take into account the fact that a good number of
volunteer firemen live on School Street). In the nineteenth century there were three sizable fires that started
in the wharf area by Cannon Square. That of April 2,
1837 ("supposed to be the work of an incendiary," said
the Providence *Journal*), destroyed nineteen houses and
damaged two more. There was no fire engine, though
one was bought soon after. Men of the village formed a
chain and passed buckets of water from the harbor. Wet
blankets were spread on endangered buildings. In one
burning building, Mrs. Hancox handed her eleven-
month-old son, Nathaniel, to some person in the heat of
the action, and for a while afterwards he couldn't be
found. He was eventually discovered, well wrapped up,

lying in the yard of the Hyde House a bit further along Water Street. Nathaniel grew up to be a keen wit.

Open fires and sooty chimneys produced unwanted blazes, and when they occurred it was imperative for all the men to turn out. The first fire engines were pumped by hand—forty men were needed to work some of them —and they had such names as Niagara, Deluge, Damper, Fountain, Annihilator, Phoenix, and Excelsior. The three Stonington companies are still called Pioneers, Steamers, and Neptunes. John Ericsson, the engineer who later designed the Civil War vessel *Monitor*, built the first mobile steam engine in the United States in 1840. According to Edwin Mitchell, a historian of American villages, the first fire engine in Norwich, not far from Stonington, was built in 1788 as a collaborative effort between a coachmaker and a clockmaker.

These days the number of serious fires in the village is small. Central heating has cut down the risk engendered by coal stoves and kerosene space heaters. Most alarms now sound for grass fires, started along the edge of the railroad tracks by sparks from overheated bearings. Late winter and spring seem to be the dry grass seasons. A few years ago a railroad fire got going on Wamphassuc Point in March and burned off half a dozen acres, menacing several houses and a lovely old barn before it was brought under control. Now and then some woman cooking breakfast sets fire to a pan, which in turn sets fire to grease collected in a flue, but these fires usually burn themselves out just as the Pioneers, Steamers, or Neptunes roll up with their splendid, gleaming appliances. The two-hoot all-clear sounds soon after the original alarm, and most people feel a slight surge of disappointment.

This desire to see a blaze, to see flames in charge, and to see something consumed is perhaps because we want reminders of the sudden ending to which all things are liable; or is perhaps an atavistic pleasure at seeing fire itself, an element we don't often have contact with these days, but which once burned brightly in hearths and the mouths of caves, and which we have tamed to glow in coils beneath our cooking pots or behind steel doors in our furnaces. And perhaps it is from a need for sheer melodrama, people running, red trucks speeding with men hanging on, and shouts of stand back, mind the hose, turn it on now. Geysers of smoke and jets of water and the sounds of windows breaking. Certainly in the village, when the alarm sounds, people turn out. Most kitchens have pinned up in a prominent spot the list of alarm signals—two-three is the corner of Water and Wall, one-seven the boat yard, etc. When the first hoot is heard, there is silence in every house while the following blasts are counted. Then they appear on their front steps and hasten to the spot, nodding as they recognize one another: Tom Powell, the insurance man, the Stones and the Bianchinis, Maria McVitty, Henry Chapin, Tricia Dodson, and without fail Evie Cole. Having survived the

1938 hurricane, Mrs. Cole seems to have retained a keen taste for disasters—or it may simply be that having spent much of her real-estate career in promoting Stonington as the St. Tropez of New England, she feels more responsible for its property than the average villager. At any rate, when the fire signal sounds she is soon on her way, always well-groomed and wearing her pearls. Tricia Dodson said she met Evie Cole one night en route to a fire on the town dock; a shed full of lobster pots was blazing. In the light of a street lamp Tricia thought Mrs. Cole looked not her usual self—something was different. Then, realizing why, she asked, "Evie, where are your pearls?" Mrs. Cole's hand flew to her neck. She said, "Oh my!" and dashed home to put them on before heading for the fire again.

The fire house still has some of the characteristics of a clubhouse where men get together in the course of drills and the maintenance of fire equipment. But the average age of the volunteers seems to have risen in the last decades. Television and the private car (which enables a man to get out of the village for work and entertainment) have sapped the attractions of the fire house as a home away from home. And the fact that many able-bodied village men work in factories elsewhere has reduced the numbers of volunteers on call. At an alarm one morning last year, only one man turned out. This was Andy Perry, from the lumberyard. Alone he manned a fire truck and drove it to the scene. Fortunately it was only a grass fire, but Andy had an arduous hour wrestling with the hose before he put it out.

The fact that ordinary citizens who aren't firemen feel bound to turn out and participate in a fire isn't particularly welcomed by the Pioneers, Steamers, and Neptunes. People sometimes try to help, and help too much. In a serious kitchen fire not long ago the firemen turned out in strength (it was a good hour, nine p.m., when most men were at home and not yet in bed). When they reached the fire they found their access impeded by a lady from a nearby house, decently attempting to remove some of her neighbor's prized possessions from the threatened holocaust. A Hepplewhite table blocked the back door. A teak chest was athwart the garden path. In the heat and hubbub commands were shouted abruptly. Tempers flared. Was there or was there not an accusation of looting? Umbrage was taken. Language got stronger. The helpful lady was removed forcibly by the fire police and driven off swearing to the Pawcatuck lockup. The fire was soon put out. Friends arrived to release the lady from prison and—since her fires were still burning rather warmly—this took them a little longer.

The all-clear, two long blasts of the siren, is also sounded nightly as a test signal at seven p.m. It is used by many parents as a signal for bedtime for small children. But the signal is not always exactly at seven, and now and then seems to be forgotten altogether. There was a period a few years ago when it got later and later every night, until at last, when it was sounding at a quarter to eight, the fireman in charge of blowing the siren was asked how he got his time. He said, "Oh, I stop by Freddy's jewelry shop down on Water Street and look at his window clock." That seemed fair enough. However, someone thoughtfully asked Freddy how he set his clock. Freddy said, "I generally go by the fire whistle."

～§ 17 §～

A STRANGER COMING HERE from another world or another country would be surprised by one feature of life in the village, and that is the number of parties. It is as if we don't really see enough of each other, or feel guilty about the extent and depth of our relationships, and are thus compelled to invite one another to these ceremonies at which, encouraged by alcohol, we attempt to bridge the gaps and chasms. Summer parties are a trifle dangerous in this respect. A room or garden may be full of sparkling, not very familiar people of similar age, drinking and conversing, and it may suddenly be easier for a woman to say, "God, I'm bored with my life," or a man to say, "You're very beautiful"—causing a gap to be excitingly closed between two people who, half an hour before, may not have been aware a gap existed. In the winter season we are already better acquainted with one another, and there is an integration of ages and professions, neighbors and non-neighbors, and like and unlike. At the older Dodsons', for instance, at a party before Christmas, there will be naval officers, engineers, lawyers, tree surgeons, teachers, photographers, old

ladies, college girls, a young lobsterman, and some visitor—a British art dealer, a Portuguese girl who works
for a travel agency in Washington—whose questions
perform a sort of squeezing, compacting action, out of
which we become uniformly identifiable as villagers, inhabitants of a specific place. The Dodson parties, moreover, have a family core. There are sons and daughters,
sons-in-law and daughters-in-law, grandchildren me-
andering at knee height, and eight or nine dogs of different breeds and pedigrees, the mongrels in mongrel
fashion making up in friendliness what they lack in re-
finement. When dog-owners leave the village for a week
or so and need a home for their animal, they call Evelyn
Dodson, who never makes excuses.

The kind of hospitality which is natural to the Dodsons (which is not to say that it isn't hard work or not
well considered) is perhaps exceptional anywhere, but
for me the Dodsons are associated with a large white
house, 21 Main Street, in Stonington, and for that reason
the village itself is that much more hospitable. I know
that coming in through the front door and edging
through a crowd of people Evie will be there and will
put her cheek up to be pecked, and then John Dodson
will lead me to the table by the grand piano and make
me a drink and say in his growly voice, "Now you know
where it is, make the next one for yourself, and get one
for Evie while you're at it." Which is a way of giving
you the freedom of his house. And the house itself is the

proper scene for them, with a large welcoming entrance hall and a long living room with a big fireplace, piano, many paintings, several sofas, sidetables, and chairs—a room which can accommodate two or three interrelated conversations or a single noisy party. Behind the living room is a small library, with a Pennsylvania Dutch iron fireplace, and to one side the dining room, with a formal, polished mahogany table. There, at the end of what one had supposed to be merely a cocktail party, silver tureens full of good things blossom under Mrs. Rita's plump hands. There is always a suggestion that the Dodsons are not only doing something they can afford and are clever at but are themselves having a good time.

On Christmas Eve we generally go there at six. Santa Claus in the naturally rotund shape of Captain Ramsbotham or the padded form of Frank Lynch makes his appearance at six thirty, ho-ho-hoing down the stairs. This scares some children, thrills others, and causes a perceptive few to ask, "Why is Santa Claus wearing a mask, Daddy?" Santa gives small presents to the children, and the Dodsons exchange what they call made-presents: wine racks, Rube Goldberg painting machines, lamp shades, and (stretching the definition of "made-present" a little) a '48 Oldsmobile, towed by Bill d'Amico from Whewells' car dump for Keith (who at this point is fourteen) to pull apart and paint. After dinner there is dancing and singing, or at least Margaret Davol dances, and Peter Tripp sings, and I turn the pages while Mary plays Gilbert and Sullivan on the piano, and at some point in the festivities John Dodson goes over to Betty Henderson, a somewhat unbending matron, and whisks her skirt up around her neck, saying jovially, "Well, at least you're wearing pants tonight."

Just before Christmas we went to a surprise birthday party Matthew Verney gave his wife. Laura said later she suspected something, but she didn't realize what until she came down into a room already half full of friends and neighbors. Matt had made spaghetti sauce that afternoon at Mary Tripp's—he said he'd peeled the mushrooms, not realizing that you didn't have to. Two women friends of Laura's brought ice cream and cake. There were several bottles of rum and three gallons of wine. Peter Tripp, Dick Baum, Matt, and I managed to bring over Mary Tripp's small upright piano. Hickory logs burned in the Franklin stove. The spaghetti was properly *al dente*. The young women did a can-can, wearing men's shoes and high kicking, and the Verney's living-room floor went up and down at least six inches in three-second periods. Henry Chapin stood beside the Franklin with a kitchen fire extinguisher, sure that at any moment the beams would collapse and Franklin stove, upright piano, and can-can dancers would crash together into the cellar; then the conflagration would begin. (Henry was perhaps affected by the condition of his own beams, which I, as an old tenant of his, once told him are nearly eaten through, and he insists will last his lifetime—to which I have no response to make, since I hope his life will be very long.) We sang songs. Martin Buber says: "Community is where community happens" —in city, town, or village, in a street or a bus, in an air-raid shelter, a lifeboat, or a concert hall; and on this occasion among assorted people some of whom in other circumstances might have considered themselves not at all the sort of people who indulged in public singing. Later we carried the upright and Johnny Dodson, Jr., home.

It was somewhat different when the young Dodsons emigrated to Australia. Then a party was held in the old Baptist Church on Main Street, and just about everyone who came the young Dodsons knew. There were people from Pennsylvania and Canada, Pawcatuck and New London, and a great deal of Stonington. Mr. Schepis came, and Frankie Keane, and Mr. Siegel. Harry Scheel, the yacht designer, made a funny, tear-jerking speech. Presents were presented, and Johnny and Tricia and a lot of people cried. And when the young Dodsons were gone we had a less confident feeling about the village for a while. After all, they had decided that life—even life in Sydney, the most American of Australian cities—working for a big engineering firm—big business, rather than the family boat yard—might be more promising than life in Stonington. A segment had been removed from the orange, a large slice carved from the pie, and it was briefly possible to look in and see some of the things we were made of. Hadn't Johnny, leaving, sold his house to an elderly retired couple? Didn't the village have a middle-aging effect—a concern with property, with social obligations on too minor a scale? Wasn't there a world elsewhere in which great things were to be competed for? Wasn't this a serene backwater in which it was hard to feel even the eddies of the mainstream? For a few weeks, until the scar began to heal, the natives of the microcosm found the macrocosm's Medusa-like face strangely appealing.

On the afternoon of New Year's Day, Mrs. Hoppin gives a party. The printed invitation, decorated with engraved red and green holly, says: "Kay Hoppin invites you to mulled wine and candlelight." Mrs. Hoppin, a widow, had been principal of a private school in Manhattan, and her husband—judging by the teak chests and carved screens in the house—had had connections with the Orient. By five o'clock the candles are lit and the house is full. A year or so ago we arrived in an ice storm and, leaving the car, grasped the nearest fence and edged along it to Mrs. Hoppin's open gate, wobbled up the steps, and joined our immediate predecessors in the tiny hall, struggling to remove boots and galoshes. There was another jam on the stairs. People said hullo and happy new year as they made their way to and from the bedrooms where they'd been ordered to leave their coats. Then at the foot again they met Kay Hoppin, a small gray sparrow of a lady, who said, "Ah, there you are, now you're going to have to meet my nephew, he's in the front room by the fire, clever fellow, but wait—you haven't got some wine yet, have you? Well, fight your way through!"

So into the dining room. There most of the space seemed to be taken up by an oval table. Most of the table was taken up by silver plates and trays covered with scones, hors d'oeuvres, and hot home-made doughnuts the size of golf balls, and an ornate silver tea service, behind which Mrs. Hoppin had conscripted one of the first-arriving ladies to sit and pour. But this task was clearly an honor, one felt, seeing how the appointed pourer sat, beaming, amid the gleaming utensils and fine china, with attendant ladies ready to pass lemon, sugar, cream, and the little jug of rum, and also ready, the moment the pourer seemed to tire or the hostess decided to change the hand at the wheel, to move into the upright chair behind the teapot.

There was very little room left around the table. Shoulder to shoulder, a string of people stood against the sideboard and bookcases, bunched a little in the corner by the wine bowl. One found oneself, cup in hand, packed alongside someone one might not know or rarely saw, and such was the congestion and perhaps such the antique atmosphere, with the candles flickering in wall brackets, that it was not as hard as one might have expected to manufacture conversation, a bit jerry-built at first but soon more enthusiastic and inquisitive, to the person blockaded there in the same confinement as oneself—finding that Mrs. Davies under her bitter exterior had wit; that the reclusive millionaire loved trees, and loved talking about trees; and that a woman who always seemed such a frivolous person had just returned from three months' hospital work in Laos. The wine had an undoubted warming effect, though more than two cups left one feeling both mulled and spiced. John Dodge's creased sour look became a creased, almost cheerful look. The vicar, who had wondered fearfully what to do if violent black-power advocates came and demanded reparations from whitey in Stonington, put a friendly arm round the shoulders of a black exchange student from Zambia. And Dr. Haliday, who was then still alive, and whose patience was daily tried by one or other of the people collected in these rooms, now beamed at them all as he discussed with Margot, my wife, his youth in Canada, his war service in New Guinea among head-hunters, and—since she shared his interest in Charles Darwin—various aspects of evolution and the survival of the fit.

Leaving Mrs. Hoppin's, boots, coats, and gloves donned again, leaving the firelight and candlelight, wishing our hostess goodnight and a prosperous New Year, which she returned while simultaneously welcoming a group of late arrivals ("It's thinning out a little in the back. Now, boots here, coats upstairs. Then you'll have to meet my nephew in the front room. You're wise to come late . . ."), and stepping out into the icy, windy night, we were, I felt, perhaps a slightly higher animal than we sometimes showed.

❦ 18 ❧

WALKING DOWN WATER STREET the other night, past the open windows in the ground floor of the Plax division of Monsanto, I heard three men of the second shift singing "America the Beautiful." They were singing loudly, over the noise of their lathes and drill presses: ". . . for spacious skies . . . from sea to shining sea." Perhaps it was the only song all three of them knew some words of. At any rate, they sang in a joshing sort of way, as if they didn't want to sound too nuttily patriotic or affectionate, like grown men singing Happy Birthday to You to their mothers.

In fall my daughter Liz brings home from school a mimeographed form to be filled up. I have to say whether I work for any Federal agency or serve in the armed forces, such as the Navy or Coast Guard, in which case the school system gets a subsidy from the government. Quite a lot of men in the village are so employed. There are submariners and Coast Guard officers, hospital corpsmen and young doctors serving their time. Many men work at Electric Boat in Groton, building and repairing submarines. (They drive to and from work in car pools.) Other large employers of villagers are Pfizer, also in Groton, a chemical firm; Yardney, in Pawcatuck, which makes electric batteries, transformers and fuel cells; and Cottrell's, also in Pawcatuck, a manufacturer of printing machinery. Closer at hand is the mill: the American Velvet Company. It is on Bayview Avenue, in the across-the-tracks section of the village, with a green water tower and a tall brick chimney, and surrounded by "mill houses" which in time have been fancied up and made different from one another by various kinds of siding and trim—the residents of the area are sufficiently house-proud to complain frequently about the sooty fallout from the mill chimney. I once made a list of the occupations in a textile mill. There were beamers, warpers, slashers, doffers, carders, combers, lappers, drawers, rovers, twisters, mule-spinners, frame-spinners, weavers, winders, reelers, spoolers, loom-fixers, slubbers, and trimmers. It was the mill that brought in many of the Portuguese to work here, and the Wimpfheimers, who still own it, rewarded their employees with free lots to build houses on. Today in the mill you can still hear the deafening clatter of looms—the sound that was most typical of nineteenth-century New England industry; but the employees also have such twentieth-century privileges as profit-sharing. The Wimpfheimers, moreover, take seriously their role as leaders of local industry, and without any flamboyance provide much of the backing for "good causes," such as the Community Center.

On the Point, the big trucks coming and going to

Plax annoy some of the householders on Water Street and Main Street, but they also remind us that there actually is a place in the village where men and women earn their living. (Joe Costa, who used to own my house—he bought it in the twenties for twelve hundred dollars and sold in the thirties for twenty-three hundred, having turned it into a two-family house—worked in the Plax building when it was the Atwood Machine shop; he was a foreman there and when Atwood's closed was paid off without a pension.) The husband of Mrs. Cunha, the elderly lady on Omega Street who sometimes babysits for us, was a machinist at Atwood's and died on the job there. Nowadays every morning at five past eight, Manuel Narcizzi—having just finished the night shift at Plax —walks up School Street to his house, lunch box under his arm.

For several hundred years there were ship yards in the village. Boats were built on Long Point by Thomas Stanton's sons long before there were any houses. In the nineteenth century schooners were the trucks of the time, carrying cargoes from one place to another. There was also need for whalers, sealers, passenger packets, and privateers. Behind the two breakwaters the coasting vessels sheltered from gales and waited for the wind to change. On small sloops Stonington men voyaged as far as Antarctica and as close as Block Island. The Stonington Boat Works at the foot of Church Street built fishing draggers through World War II, and continued to build yachts for some years afterwards. Now the yachts can be more cheaply and better built in Finland or Hong Kong. Peter Tripp builds an occasional dory in his workshop on Ash Street, and the lobstermen order their lobster boats in hull form from Nova Scotia and complete them themselves. Many of the craftsmen work at the Mystic Seaport marine museum, restoring and repairing the ships and boats that have been preserved from the days of working sail. Others, in these prosperous days of leisure sailing, work for Dodson's, maintaining the yachts which are out of the water seven months of the year. Although fiberglass is the material of which most modern yachts are made, wooden boats continue to be most highly prized by those who have the time or the money to keep them up, and at a yard like Dodson's the vocabulary which pertains to wooden boats is still unromantically but most practically in use: futtocks, carlins, breasthooks, coamings, rabbeting, caulking—though even at Dodson's there may be only one or two who could rattle off the names of the different irons used for laying the caulking cotton in the seams between the planks to make them watertight: creasing, dumb, bent, spike, sharp, reefing, and reaming. They say that some boats, whose planking is rotten and whose fastenings are sick, are held together by the quality of their caulking.

On shore the material of the age is metal. Cars, appliances, fittings of one sort or another—they all need welding, braizing, hammering, greasing, and tuning. The village supports one garage that seems to do well and two more that change hands fairly often. The two car dealers, one Ford, one Plymouth, moved last year from the village to Route 1, where more motorists presumably pass by and see the new cars on display, and where they have become part of the congestion-making ribbon development that is taking place between Westerly and Mystic. (The town plan, made ten years ago, needs updating.) The village has a welding shop for the repair of industrial equipment; a small machine shop where three men sitting at well-lit benches do precision work in a spotless, studio-like building; and Buddy Jacob's marine chandlery, where the fishermen get their winches, hoists, and otter boards repaired—Buddy, the harbor master, also repairs broken ironing boards and children's tricycles, for a change or for kindness, certainly not for much money. The village keeps two appliance men busy, one specializing in refrigerators and the other in washing machines.

It is generally a good place for getting things done. Although a few people complain that contractors, carpenters, plumbers, and electricians are hard to get, they are people who have never tried to get a plumber in piratical New York or a gas serviceman in nationalized England. The telephone works well, the electricity flows without much more than a short annual breakdown (thick ice and snow on the power lines, or a traffic accident which knocks down a utility pole). The mains water is expensive, but it is the exception. Compared to other places in the urban northeast, the taxes are not particularly high, though they are rising. Services of all kinds tend to cost more as places increase in size—in the case of public services such as police and education, the relative cost in an American city of a million is roughly twice what it is in a town of twenty-five thousand. Other benefits we enjoy are the secondary services provided by men moonlighting from (or simply supplementing) their regular jobs. They fulfill the traditional function of the hired man, who swept the yard, cut the grass, painted the fence, put out the garbage cans, and generally "kept an eye on things" when the owner was away. Several men on School Street do these sorts of jobs for people on Main and Water Streets. They often do an even neater job of trimming, say, Miss Stimson's hedge than they do of their own. One or two men have turned all these part-time jobs into a full-time occupation, and do nothing other than drive school buses, put the flags up at the post office, sweep the leaves in Cannon Square, polish the doorknobs at the bank, wash the windows at the library, and shovel snow. One man—a successful building contractor who in the evenings tends bar at the Harbor View—gives the impression that moonlighting for him is not a way of supplementing his income but of providing himself with company.

The village also shelters a number of men who don't

work. In some cases it's a matter of ordinary retirement from business or the armed services. In others, the retirement has come earlier. There are refugees from oppressive families and dominant mothers, drop-outs from the urban rat race, and men who simply want to be somewhere other than the spot where the family fortunes were made that enable them to live in the village. The village is their refuge. They have their small routines, their boats, their gardens, their visits to their post-office box, their correspondence with family lawyers, trustees, and stockbrokers. Some of them have pick-up trucks in which they drive around on their errands, looking very busy. One of them, David Vallie, is busily writing a philosophical treatise on the art of keeping busy. Several speculate in local real estate. They make long lists of all the jobs they have to do. They have hobbies, like making telescopes, in which they become a good deal more perfectionist than they would be if they were doing the job for a living. Personally, I don't think the new age of leisure which is rumored to be almost upon us is to be feared—at least once one's got over the existentialist dread of twelve hours of one's own to make free use of. Some of these men are on the wagon, and others have trouble postponing the first cocktail of the day; perhaps the Protestant ethic "work we must" is still an influence here, a ruinous taskmaster. But most of these men prove that work in the old-fashioned sense doesn't redeem people. On the contrary, it can make the unimaginative even more so; it can make the earnest and ambitious thoroughly obnoxious. Stonington has in its leisured class many doubtful men who clearly don't have a simple goal and don't know the answers, and I find this doubt —sometimes radiating through an assured façade—likeable and disarming.

◦§ 19 §◦

THE WORST MONTHS of the year begin in mid-January. It is suddenly very cold. "Fourteen below in Ledyard this morning," says someone in Frankie Keane's news office. It is zero here. Sea smoke rises on the water this side of Sandy Point, and there's ice on the far side as far as Watch Hill. A clear ice-blue sky, which one can take for a while but which becomes merciless before long. The wind begins to blow, snowstorms lose their earlier fascination, and the furnace chugs away in a dollar-consuming attempt to keep warmly abreast of things. Those who can afford the time or money take vacations at this season—the Chapins are in Greece, Evie Cole is in Italy, the Dodsons are in Algeria, and the landowners in the country are off on world cruises, bumping into each other in Hong Kong and Gibraltar. The richer sailors have flown to the Caribbean and the more prosperous shopkeepers are in Florida and the Bahamas, making up for their busy summers in the north and returning with deep tans; though last year Mr. Hirsch of Camacho's delicatessen came back pink and disgruntled; he'd got badly sunburned the first day in Miami and spent the rest of his Florida week in bed.

Those of us left feel obliged to keep things going. We keep the doctor's waiting room crowded, especially in the in-between weather which brings on the flu and brings to the doctor people who are actually sick, and not only the usual quota of children having shots, world travelers getting inoculations, and young mothers having prenatal examinations. My own health is generally good, touch wood—though I'm not immune to the bugs which whizz around the village in miniature epidemics of virus colds or stomach infections. There are some weeks when half the population seems to have diarrhea, or the Stonington runs, as Johnny Dodson, Jr., used to call it. Moreover, once a winter I decide I am really ill. I have a day or so of aches and fever, perhaps psychosomatic in origin but—as I have to insist to my family—nonetheless painful on that account. My wife is furious, partly from apprehension, when I am ill, and begins to look after me with sweet wifeliness only when I am about to get up, feeling better. In bed, I lie full of Vitamin C, aspirins, lemon juice and honey, and a good portion of self-pity. With a temperature running at a little over a hundred and one I can read Pound's *Cantos* and enjoy the ragbag of Anglo-Saxon seafaring, Provençal troubadouring, Italian petty-princing, midwestern nineteenth-century economics, and Chinese lyricism:

> *E lo Sordels si fo di Mantovana,*
> *Son of a poor knight, Sier Escort,*
> *And he delighted himself in chançons*

And mixed with the men of the court
And went to the court of Richard Saint Boniface
And was there taken with love for his wife
  Cunizza, da Romano
That freed her slaves on a Wednesday—

and the whole thing runs well enough while my temperature remains steady; but then it suddenly rises a little and I fall back on the pillow with delirious visions: a gigantic bridge, designed by Henry Fuseli and sponsored by Robert Moses, spreads across Fishers Island Sound and plants its concrete feet on the village. Over it hover a cloud of smoke and a smell like peat or marijuana burning, while square-rigged ships brace their yards to fetch through the cut between Napatree and Sandy Point, where there is less than two feet of water at mean low tide . . .

To be a doctor in the village is to put under the glass a good assortment of specimens. "Oh, I could tell you some stories!" said the late Dr. Haliday, with a rueful and impatient laugh—though of course he never did. I imagine that you have to like knowing people better than they know themselves; know when to humor them and when to be tough with them. (This is probably partly why it took nearly a year for Stonington to get another general practitioner. Most young doctors seem to want to work in a group practice on a superhighway interchange and reduce their intimate responsibilities to a minimum.) As a village doctor, I would be scared that one of the notable hypochondriacs (and in fact there are whole families of hypochondriacs) would actually have a serious complaint and die, leaving one with the memory of having said, "Take two aspirins and go to bed." Dr. Haliday charged six dollars for an office visit and ten for a house call; he turned out in the middle of the night, grumpily but without much delay, especially if a child seemed urgently ill. He was moved by childbirth, and had tears in his eyes on the three occasions he came to the hospital lobby to bring me the good news. He didn't like antibiotics much but prescribed them for those who really needed them or those who were convinced that antibiotics were what they needed, and could afford them. It is a short step across the Square from the doctor's office to the Corner Drug Store. There, after typing up the prescription label in his back room, Eddie Bessette comes forth with a small jar of ten high-powered capsules and firmly looks the customer in the eye as he murmurs (in a voice that is not his but that of Messrs. Upjohn, Merck, Pfizer, and Lilly): "That will be nine dollars and eighty-five cents."

In John Evelyn's days, the seventeenth century, people coped with their severe illnesses by letting blood. They had leeches applied, which sucked up some of the precious fluid. I don't know how many people it killed, but judging from his diary it never seemed to do Evelyn much harm. In the village the bloodmobile turns up at this time of year, as if to tap a traditional source, and

those who feel generous with their blood or simply feel it
would do them good to get rid of some (because it feels
congested, curdled, needs to be thinned out a little; perhaps being indoors and all the central heating has something to do with it) turn up in the basement of St. Mary's
Church. Ladies from the village are there in white
smocks, arranging the donors in neat rows of chairs,
handing out orange juice and leading them to the nurse
who tests a drop of blood. An elderly out-of-town
doctor (who looks about to have a heart attack) checks
one's blood pressure. There are ambiguous questions to
answer about foreign travel, really designed to find out if
one has been to Mexico or Africa recently and thus
come in contact with hepatitis and tsetse flies. Assuming
one is nervous, the goodwill ladies make nervous-making
conversation about one's wife and children. One has a
view across the room of ladies' shoes sticking out from
under sheets hiding their outstretched legs, and plastic
bags hanging from the sides of the high beds, filling with
black liquid. What if—what if a vampire society has
taken over, and this is a wicked conspiracy to drain the
blood of the entire village? That face, suddenly ap-
pearing over a portable screen, looks like Alfred Hitch-
cock's. What if . . . ? But one's arm is taken, one is
being led to a bed. I take a reassuring look at the statue
of St. Peter that I last saw in the Holy Ghost parade,
pastel blue and pink and gold, smiling. A high-breasted
nurse in her late thirties rolls my shirt sleeve up and says

with suggestive flattery, "I can tell you work out of doors. Now, you're really going to give it to me, aren't you?" *Jab.* But instead of staying there and holding my hand she's gone to another customer, and a high-school girl who looks as if she's about to faint is dispatched to keep an eye on the tubes and connections. I make noblest-Roman conversation, not without a touch of self-interest, asking as the life ebbs out of me: "How many pints do I hold, anyway?"

The high-school girl goes whiter than ever. "Gee," she says, "I don't know. We get to the human body next semester. Just now we're on ferns and mosses."

The after-effects are worth it. Having survived the protocol of semi-invalidism, the helping hand, the luke-warm cup of coffee, a stale doughnut and a small red heart-shaped pin, I feel quite high for an hour or so—lightened in mind and body. "You know they're not to drink or exert themselves for two or three hours," says someone to my wife, come to drive me away, apparently because people do want to exert themselves and feel fantastically amorous. I chase my wife upstairs but she evades me. I collapse on the bed, singing an old school song whose words, until this moment, I had no idea I remembered.

In the Village

I HALF-REMEMBER A POEM of Roy Campbell's: ". . . in winter, when the leaves depart, nature, the paragon of art" takes hold. Ice and snow provide compensations of the season. On Silvia's Pond, buried in the woods just north of the village, the ice forms maybe a foot thick. There are long rifts and cracks, but there's no sense of movement and no view of water underneath. Now and then there are dull detonations as the ice expands; the sound reverberates from the middle toward the shore, and echoes off the rocky cliffs, two to twenty feet high, which mostly surround the pond. At the edges, the ice is faulted and delaminated, like plywood where one or two veneers have peeled or split to expose a void beneath. The ice has bubbles of air in it and different colors—or colors as different as those in diamonds and sapphires. Here and there it is frosted with snow.

This is the pond that gave the family and descendants of Frank G. Silvia, Stonington's first Portuguese settler, much of their living from the 1840's to 1947. Mandy Lindberg, who lives near one end of the pond, remembers an ice house at either end until just after World War II. Apparently the first man to try to make money out of ice in America was one Frederick Tudor, of Boston, who in 1805 shipped a cargo of ice from Fresh Pond, Cambridge, to Martinique, in the French West Indies. The venture was a total loss. However, Mr. Tudor persevered, and soon other people joined in running success-

(187)

ful ice businesses. In 1860 (according to Edwin Mitchell) the price on a family rate in Boston was $5 for the season of May to October, for 9 pounds a day, $8 for 15 pounds a day, and $12 for 24 pounds a day. The ice was first cut with axes and then the cakes were poled along through canals in the ice to a loading place, from which a horse-drawn sled carried them to the ice house. As time went on the icemen developed other implements—a horse-drawn scraper which cleared snow ice from the surface, a horse-drawn plough with which the ice was marked for cutting in five-foot squares, and a horse-drawn cutter which split up the ice. The ice house generally had its door on the north side, and stood under the shade of a tree. Stored in sawdust, the ice lasted a year.

We sit on the rocks at the edge of Silvia's Pond and put on our skates, and then push off on a reconnaissance. On a weekend afternoon in January a dozen or so skaters are there. A bonfire burns on the little island two thirds of the way to the north end, and someone is roasting hot dogs. Where the Lindbergs' land slopes down to the pond edge and frozen mud meets frozen water, a few old aluminum garden chairs have been left; these make splendid training devices. You can push them ahead of yourself, and they provide support without too much inertia. You can acquire the proper forward lean and movement of the feet, and pretty soon push the chair aside and keep on going. Learning to skate as an

adult is one way to recover the earlier thrills of learning
to walk, or swim. The pond is half a mile long, and there
is plenty of room for both duffers and experts—for children like my daughter Anny, who takes as much pleasure in sliding on her bottom as on her feet, and for
ladies in elegant skating costumes like Mrs. Hurlburt,
who moves effortlessly and gracefully across the ice,
now and then spinning to a smiling stop for a moment of
conversation; and then skates on—as at a cocktail party
where you don't have to make excuses such as needing
another drink. The mechanics are fluid here. You can go
off on your own and still show off. You can skate into
the sun or away from it. The island is something to be
skated around. You can sit by the bonfire, take off your
skates, and warm your feet. On the way back through
the woods we pick up logs for the fire at home.

After a heavy snowstorm in the village the two
steep, hilly blocks of Cliff Street and High Street, behind
the drug store, are blocked with sawhorses at top and
bottom and reserved for sledding. Rival gangs of children snowball each other on the way up and down.
They collide on purpose, they fall off, they go over
bumps they've made of heaped-up snow. Snowsuited
small children go down with wide-open eyes and
mouths, sitting between their mothers' legs; red stocking
caps and red cheeks; frosted breath in the air; snow in
your boots; wet gloves, numb hands; the straighter you
steer, the faster you go, flat out, the only problem is to

stop before you reach the curb on the far side of Elm Street with a thud. A friend from Noank, a nearby village, said he envied us our streets reserved for sledding. They'd tried to do the same in Noank but had failed when faced with one citizen who insisted on his right to bring his car to his own door, halfway up their hill. Our residents' public spirit may reside in the fact that the hills are short and the few houses have front doors on other streets—in which case we should congratulate the house-builders for their foresight.

Other diversionary activities go on indoors. A select membership subscribes to the Winter Assemblies, a series of after-dinner dances held in several of Stonington's statelier homes. The subscription ($25 per couple for three dances) covers the cost of music, a barman, ice, and mixes—liquor, you bring your own. A three-piece band (which has either sunk to this level or for evident reason never climbed above it) plays from nine till midnight, the three men smiling determinedly as if their bared teeth might take one's mind off wrong notes, dull rhythm, and stale melodies. The assemblies form the only chance one generally has of seeing at this season the semi-retired people who are to be found on the Club porch in summer, eating social lunches, or of meeting the local naval folk, whose intelligence often seems brushed over with a thick layer of opacity. Perhaps this is the result of a life geared to rank and discipline; of having to hide your opinions, even if they are bright and correct, from your superior officers; and then, when a career of keeping your mouth tactfully shut has brought you to the command position, of having to hide your feelings from the men under your command.

In the village, when an invitation says six o'clock, many people arrive at five minutes to. But for the assemblies, coming on from private dinner parties, they tend to turn up a little late. We created a sensation once by arriving at an assembly at five minutes past nine, bringing the welcoming committee in a rush from their dinner table to the front door to greet us. We'd had spaghetti at home.

A theater club, the Stonington Players, provides a wide-based membership with some alleviation of the February blues. Struggles for power in the steering group are matched by fierce guerrilla work in the play-selection committee. However, which play they do actually matters little, be it a comic melodrama set in a Bucks County farmhouse or a comic murder mystery set in a mansion on Cape Hatteras—the most decrepit, dated Broadway drama becomes a winged vehicle for the village cast, at least in the amused eyes of those who've come to watch the performances of people well known in other guises. Perhaps "other guises" is not accurate—the forte of most local actors is to be themselves a little more leadenly or self-consciously than usual. A few rise above this, exaggerating their own characteristics rather than assuming those intended by the playwright. And this is the pleasure: to see Captain Ramy Ramsbotham being Ramy Ramsbotham to the nth while dressed up as a Greek warrior, or John Dodson, Sr., playing the part of a slow-moving, shambling, inarticulate and indomitable Negro butler, giving us the quintessence of John Dodson, Sr.

The production is also a play within a play, or a play enveloping a play. Phones ring all the time. There are feuds and alliances. Some people are doing all the work for which other people will get the credit. So some people say. Men who can't be got to paint the bathroom ceiling put in long hours making scenery. Women neglect their kitchens and children. It's called the magic of the theater. In fact, it is amazing how theatrical these people suddenly get. The young mother of four whom we've always taken for a pretty but rather suburban girl wears make-up all day long and looks ravishing; she has stardust in her eyes. The juvenile lead is quite possibly madly in love with her. The lady who gets murdered in the last act is to be seen in Roland's Market throwing exaggeratedly suspicious glances at her fellow-shoppers; which one has the pistol in her pocketbook? The performance of the play itself is simply the largest in a series of waves, and if, like some ninth waves, it doesn't break with a roar but falls flat, no one seems terribly upset. Friends say: "The production was lovely." The performers are still so far removed from reality that it doesn't matter that the auditorium was half full and that

one person—unrelated to anyone in the cast—actually
had the moral courage to walk out during the intermis-
sion and not come back. Indeed, for a week or so afterwards the players can't simmer down. They continue to
hold long telephone conversations with each other, telling each other how great they were, how beautiful the
costumes and how perfect the scenery. They are already
looking forward to next year.

February is a magnifying glass. People crack open
like the clapboards of warm houses exposed to cold
winds. They feel exposed. They explode. For Louis
Varka and Jim Skidmore, two young village men, the
month of February—several years ago—became insup-
portable. Skidmore worked as a lumper on Bindloss's
dock, unloading fish from draggers. Varka, who had
formerly been a lumper, ran a fish and chips shop in
Westerly; he was the father of several small children,
one of whom, a pretty little girl called Carol, sometimes
stopped to pick up my daughter Liz on the way to
school. Skidmore lived with his parents in a neatly kept
two-family house. The Varka house was full and noisy;
out of it life seemed to pour in the shape of radio music,
family quarrels, and children, while cats and garbage littered the front yard. Meanwhile, on Bindloss's dock, the
skipper of the dragger *Glory B* had been complaining
about the handling of his fish boxes—reportedly, Skidmore or Varka was dropping the boxes and spoiling the
fish. The skipper refused to sell any more fish to Varka

for his fish and chips shop. New grudges and old animosities were piled upon each other. One December
night the mooring lines of the *Glory B* were cut, but she
was secured again before she had drifted out of the dock.

In February Margot and I were sitting late at the
dinner table when we heard a bump—it seemed close at
hand, as if one of us had hit a knee hard against a table
leg, or something heavy had fallen in the cellar. A minute later we heard the fire alarm. I hurried out, putting
on overcoat and gloves as I went. The night sky above
and beyond Plax was lit by a lavender glow. I hastened
with a number of people along Water Street, thinking
perhaps an oil tank behind Bindloss's was on fire, but the
fire trucks that were already turning up as we got there
were going down along the dock, beyond the oil tanks.
Men were running the hoses from the hydrants down to
the *Glory B*, which was blazing.

The light from the conflagration illuminated the next
dock, where I joined twenty or thirty spectators. For a
while the fire hoses didn't seem to make much impression. The *Glory B*'s pilot house, a tall box on the fore-
deck, formed a chimney through which the flames
welled from deep inside the dragger, and soon the dory,
which was perched on top of the pilot house, ready for
service as lifeboat or tender, began to burn, began to
lose a dimension, became a flat, black shape which grad-
ually folded up like a charred banana skin. Through the
seams of the hull the flames also started to show. The

Glory B appeared to be built of planks caulked with molten fire. And at last, when the hoses began to make an impact, steam was added to the smoke and flames. Steam rose with the smoke, lit from beneath, spouting above the dock with sparks and ashes.

Across the small intervening stretch of water we watched with a mixture of fascination and horror—or perhaps not so much horror as a sense of Thank God it's not my boat nor anything to do with me. Pieces of equipment floated over and were scooped up and put on the dock for someone to claim. We were in an exposed position if the fire reached the fuel tanks and she exploded, but despite this no one moved away. It was too interesting. After a time, when the fire had eaten away the caulking and the weight of water in her had become great, she began to settle. She went down very slowly, barely perceptibly. Then she was resting on the bottom, slightly heeled, with only the shell of the pilot house and the mast (with nets still hung from it) standing above the water. I went home. I wondered how it had happened, but it didn't occur to me that there might be reason to think of it as any more than a spectacular fire.

However, things went on happening during the night. In Frankie Keane's next morning I handed over my dime for a New York paper, and Frank said, giving me the local news verbally, "Well, they caught one of the two boys that did it."

"They did? One?"

"The other's dead. They got his body out at three a.m.—divers from the sub base went down for it."

Skidmore had been encountered on the dock during the fire, so the local papers said that night. He wasn't a volunteer fireman. The fire marshal asked him what he was doing there, and Skidmore muttered that he thought he'd seen his buddy Varka down on the dock half an hour before; he'd come down to look for him. Someone noticed that the arm of Skidmore's coat was singed. The police took him in to ask him a few questions, and in an hour or so he told them that, after a few drinks, he and Varka had borrowed a can of gas from a lobsterboat at the dock. Varka went below in the *Glory B* and splashed the gas around. He, Skidmore, stayed up on the dock. The next thing he knew—*boom!*

Varka had a requiem mass. The flags at the Holy Ghost, one American, one Portuguese, flew at half-staff. Skidmore went to jail on an arson charge coupled with one for murder, since in Connecticut that can be tacked on if someone got killed during the commission of a felony. However, after six months the murder charge was dropped and, perhaps because Skidmore was found to be less culpable than his friend and was thought to have been punished enough, he was given a suspended sentence. The owner of the *Glory B* died of a heart attack five weeks after the incineration of his dragger, which had been uninsured. (Later that year an enterprising New Bedford man bought the hulk, strapped canvas around it, pumped out the water and mud which had collected in it, and towed it away. We were glad to see it go.) For a while after the event, we saw strangers, sightseers in out-of-town cars, driving around the village streets, and the people in them staring at each person as they passed, clearly wondering if this was someone connected with the *Glory B* disaster. They were probably satisfied to have stared into the face of a resident of the spot where the deed was done. As for local people, it seemed that for a day or so they stayed home, indoors, unwilling to see or be seen, as they did after Kennedy was shot. In its parochial way, this was a similar intimation of the demons within.

In some the demons have a hard time getting out. The fires are internal and no less fierce. March is a bad month then, with its days of false promise, suggesting the worst is over; but wet snow and gales are still to come. And though women are supposed to be the stronger sex, living longer, able to pick up hot dishes with their bare hands, a few find this period impossible to bear. The most vulnerable seem to be well-educated, fairly clever women with numerous children, up to their necks in babies, housework, schools, meals, beds, shopping, laundry. (Several years ago two pairs of men set off to row the Atlantic—the pair that made it were paratroopers; the pair that didn't, who were lost, were journalists. It's my feeling that imagination can be a liability in some circumstances.) For some women it may be easier to break down than go on. Insanity forms a haven from the banal weariness of domestic life. Suicide is the last expression of individuality and independence. Two women we knew went out of their minds; one killed herself. Of course, this may not have anything specifically to do with village life. A city might have furnished more distractions, and on the other hand it might have been more impersonal, offering even less opportunity for friendship. But in the village tragedy is visible, and people are able to help as much as they can, at least after the fact, trying to entertain desolate husbands, and taking the children now and then.

20

WOMEN: GRACE STONE SAID, "This place is full of widows." There's no doubt that whereas men without their wives look ill or desperate, women bounce back. In Stonington the archetype is Hilda Hull, heroine of the glorious battle with the British fleet; she died in her own bed, angry with her sick body and unruffled by the enemy guns. Mr. Hull, one supposes, had departed long before. For whatever their shape—and Mrs. Stone is a plump grande-dame and Mrs. Knox is wiry, Ros McCagg is tall and Evie Cole is tiny—they are tough, the elderly women of the village. One day, walking by 52 Main Street, I looked up as usual to admire the fine gambrel roof of the Chapins' house and there was Paula Chapin, walking along the ridge of it with the sureness of a seventy-year-old mountain goat, carrying a sack full of bricks, about to clean her chimney. Mrs. Stone flies Aeroflot to Moscow to take the waters and doesn't stand any nonsense from Intourist, any more than she would from Thomas Cook or the Chinese pirates who shelled the gunboat on which, as a young bride, she accompanied her husband up the Yangtse. In her hands have swung the champagne bottles which launched ships.

Their husbands drop dead of coronaries or expire of emphysema, but these ladies continue, reminiscing at cocktail parties of Batavia and Boars Hill, running domestic trim ships and keeping exemplary gardens—being a little catty with one another about their health and their holidays, but at the last, going home and saying good night, regarding each other with respect and affection—survivors; all in the same boat together. They often seem more active and less earnest than their grandchildren.

The village is prolific in girls. In Noank, not many miles away, all the women have sons, but in Stonington it seems hard to give birth to anything other than daughters. Is it the mineral content of the water? Is it some long-term historic-psychologic-genetic effect of the Battle, whereby families fail to produce young men to be cannon fodder? But this disproportion of sexes has advantages; one is the number of babysitters. In most houses on School and Trumbull Street there are families with girls of babysitting age, say between thirteen and eighteen. Below thirteen they tend to be not altogether responsible (and their parents restrict the hours they may sit). Above eighteen they are inclined to have steady boyfriends or part-time jobs with greater status, such as checking out in a supermarket or accounting at the hardware store. However, between those ages they're often glad to get out of their own family

maelstrom and into someone else's. They're also glad of
the money, which—depending on age, experience, and
sense of duty—is fifty or seventy-five cents an hour. For
several years Mary Madeira came after school and took
my smallest daughters for a walk, or came in the evening
when we wanted to go out. She always remained rather
shy of us but was attached to the children and they to
her; she did more than she knew toward keeping us all
happy. After her succeeded a string of girls, one of them
notable for her fear of going upstairs if there were no
light on—and an inability to turn the light on. Babies
could scream for hours untended. She was rapidly succeeded by a freckled plump girl whose charms—barely
visible to me—collected to our front porch several ad-
miring boys whenever we went out. Then Friday-night
basketball games had to be taken into account when
arranging our schedule, as did Thursday-afternoon after-
school baton-twirling classes and Saturday-night dances
at the Community Center.

I sometimes wonder what effect babysitting has on
these girls: does it encourage maternal desires too soon;
does it put them off motherhood altogether? Dirty
diapers are bad enough when they belong to a child of
your own. On the other hand, it's a good way of seeing
the inside of other people's houses, of realizing that other
people live in different ways from one's own family.
Most of these girls seem to have great poise, however,
and perhaps not much curiosity. The only time I've seen

one look a bit put out was when, after a party, we carried Johnny Dodson, Jr., into his house and dumped him on the sofa from which the babysitter had just jumped up. But it may have been that the look of disapproval on her face was for Tricia, who said to us, without a second look at her husband's snoring hulk: "Thanks a lot, boys, he'll be all right there till the morning."

On the street at almost all times of the year the small girls play in several packs that sometimes band together and sometimes fight, in the old style, with champions. "Cindy Rita and Lorie Grey are going to fight down at the lighthouse!" shouts my daughter Liz, running into the house to give us this information and dashing out again, lighthouse-bound. Later, when I ask for the results, she says: "Oh, they made up." There is a great deal of "breaking friends" and making up again and not letting so-and-so play—two's company. There are games of prisoner's base and hide-and-go-seek that take place at the junction of School and Trumbull Streets, with the parked cars providing a forest of hiding places. They play school a lot and pay tribute to the success of the new math by sitting on the curbs and porches with paper and pencil, doing sums and sets. They tell each other dirty jokes, such as little Johnny in school, told by teacher to say the alphabet, recites:

ABCDEFGHIJKLMNOQRSTUVWXYZ.

Teacher says, "But Johnny, where's the P?" Johnny says, "Running down my legs." This is worth a lot of giggles on School Street. And they have songs. One that accompanies a slapping hands and clapping hands game is:

> *Oh little Frankenstein*
> *Please come and fight with me*
> *Come bring your axes three*
> *Slide down my slippery slide*
> *Into my cellar door*
> *And we'll be enemies for evermore.*
>
> *Oh little Frankenstein*
> *I cannot fight today*
> *Ain't got no axes three*
> *Ain't got no slippery slide*
> *Ain't got no cellar door*
> *Oh little Frankenstein*
> *We'll be enemies for evermore.*

When I asked Cindy Rita where she got this multi-faceted strange chant from, she said, "Elizabeth Tester who's in Donna Madeira's class learned it in Germany." Cindy—who is a year or so older than the other small girls and has a great deal of personality—is the *Capo* of the Trumbull Street juvenile Cosa Nostra.

More indigenous are the cheer-leading songs the girls sing as they swing their arms and legs and do stretches and knee-bends:

> *Madeira, Madeira,*
> *Richie Madeira, he's our man,*
> *If he can't do it, Warner can—*

In the Village

Tommy Warner, he's our man,
If he can't do it, Lambrecht can—
Peter Lambrecht, he's our man,
If he can't do it, no one can.

Meanwhile Richie Madeira, making like Joe Namath, is passing the ball fast and low over the Previtys' Pontiac to Peter Lambrecht, who just catches it, fending off the Souzas' fence with one hand.

The girls go on:

Grizzly bears, polar bears,
Ready, hep hep.

Grizzly bears, polar bears,
Short and tall.
Stonington Bears, Stonington Bears,
Best of all.

Liz gets called in for supper. She comes running, chanting:

Trick or treat,
Smell my feet,
Give me something
Good to eat.

"Who taught you *that?*"
"Cindy."

Cindy is a poet. I found a letter, written to one of a pair of boys, sons of friends, whom we brought in for a few weeks to redress the balance of population.

In the Village

> *Dear Jason,*
>   *Diane and I thought of*
> *a song like this—*
> *He's a doll, He's a dream,*
> *He's right in between.*
>   *Love,*
>   *Cindy*

Mrs. Sadie Cunha babysits for us now and then. Since she lives around the corner on Omega Street, she drops by occasionally with a jug of homemade soup and enjoys a little conversation about times past. She says, looking at the girls: "Oh, they have it good now. I can remember, we had two clean dresses and three white pinafores every week—we called them Mother Hubbards. But we went barefoot all weekend. We took our shoes off Friday night and—except for church—didn't put them on again till Monday morning."

❧ 21 ❧

IN THE MORNINGS our well-shod children walk to school. Until seventh grade, when buses take them to schools out of the village, they walk to the three-story brick building (1888) on Orchard Street, overlooking Little Narragansett Bay, and walk home again. It's a good thing. The *Times* of London not long ago reported a speech made to the British Association by Dr. Terence Lee of the Psychology Department at Dundee University. Dr. Lee isn't happy about some of the effects of primary schools being closed down in the British countryside, one effect being the increased bussing of small children. He thinks children who live near enough to walk to school operate within their own familiar "mental map," their own built-in picture of their home and school and neighborhood. He says, "Bus children, however, traverse a complex causeway between two separate maps and they cannot recross the no-man's land until the bus returns." To which I would add the observation that there are things to be done, seen, and made contact with as you walk to school—leaves to scuffle through, chestnuts to pick up, shortcuts to take through

Gregory Smith's garden and the Dodges' driveway (picking by the way a few flowers for teacher from the Millers' garden), and also—traversing the stone causeway behind the field which floods in bad weather—plenty of ways to fall and get muddy. While walking to school you can find a dead squirrel or an injured bird. You can talk to other children, play jokes on them, get chased or snubbed or insulted. You don't even *have* to walk—you can skip, or run.

After the children have been got off to school there's a short, peaceful spell—a period of trance induced by newspapers and coffee. I go up to my attic to work, and if I'm a bit slow about it Margot gets the vacuum out, which gets rid of me. The day passes, punctuated by telephone calls, occasional visitors, and regular happenings: a walk to Camacho's for a loaf of Italian bread for lunch; the oil or gas man making a delivery, or the electricity or water man coming to read a meter; and John, the mailman, opening the combination screen and storm door and throwing in the day's dispatches—a fourth-class advertising booklet, a few bills, several magazines, a free tube of toothpaste, and a letter or two. I call out: "Thanks, John," and John calls back: "You're welcome." The screen door slams. The afternoon is never long enough and is somehow cut short by the truck delivering the evening paper, the New London *Day*. The truck rumbles down School Street and screeches to a slow-down outside the Arrudas' house, where the driver pushes out a load of papers. The *Days* fall with a thud to the sidewalk; the truck speeds on downhill. Soon Russell Arruda appears, often in his base- ball suit, and starts his paper route. Paper routes, like baby- sitting, are supposed to be good training for "life," but they also bring into the family some useful money— Russell makes four dollars or so a week on thirty papers. There is still an aspect here of the times when children were economic assets, doing farm work or such domestic work as weaving, rather than economic liabilities, which is what they mostly are today.

The significance of our days is that they run on un- eventfully enough, though now and then jolted by a crisis or relieved by a happy occasion. I have been read- ing the succinct diary of Manasseh Minor, who was one of the first settlers in Stonington. The diary, full of agricultural and ecclesiastical news, reflects his concerns. In April, 1707, he was sixty, and his record for the month was:

1 I cached a fox

2 I went to Sam Perys for Cloth & Mr Carder went away to sea

3 I worked at the island

4 I had seed corn of Chisbrok

6 Captn Eldredgs chilldren were baptized & Sam Bur- ton was published

7 I went with Mr Noys to the Counsel at Lebanon

14 I came home again

15 I went to see Lidya
19 Silvistars child was buryed
21 Lidya departed this life
22 Shee was buryed
23 My wife came home again
24 wood people chos thair ofisers
26 I sold my oxen to Ephraim
27 2 sarmons & Mr Sherman preached
28 wee clared the feld of cattel
29 free mens meeting
30 Thomas Noys payd me

Elsewhere in the diary women are brought to bed and there is a great snow; the Sound is frozen across to Fishers Island. Manasseh clears a salt marsh, fences the turnip yard or the spring orchard, teaches a friend to make coverlids and goes wolf-hunting. A neighbor kills a bear. Manasseh weaves a rug. In time, with neither crescendo nor falling off, the diary simply stops.

We have a calendar pinned to the side of a cupboard by the telephone.

5 prune willows
9 library meeting
10 call O'Keefe about downstairs toilet
12 meet Ingers train at Westerly
13 feed Hills' dog
16 get tomatoes from Patsy Marshall
17 pay mortgage
18 go to Coles for drinks

20 *Poo's wedding*
21 *Anny to Dr. Dolan's for shot*
24 *firewood*
26 *Robinsons for dinner*
27 *write to Henry*

There are chores which belong to certain seasons: putting up screen windows; sharpening the lawnmower; fixing a roof leak, making sure the car has anti-freeze; planting bulbs. They can occupy an afternoon at least. Take that first calendar entry, for instance—"prune willows"; it isn't quite that brief or simple. I'm not much of a gardener. My father, home from the office for lunch, would always spend ten or fifteen minutes pottering round the edges of the lawn or standing just gazing at a flower or shrub before returning to his desk and ledgers. Youth is intolerant in its estimate of the permissible forms creation can take. But I begin to see now that it is an act of imagining or helping into existence many sorts of art and many kinds of life. I have found in our garden that, as in art, the act can occasionally be negative: to get things to grow, it is necessary to hoe and weed and chop other things away. It is necessary to cut back the willow trees that Mr. Browning planted a dozen years ago at the end of his long garden. They have now grown wide and tall and hang out over our smaller plot, causing a black blight on plants underneath. Yet the trees, with soft green leaves and thin pliant boughs, are beautiful. In summer they create an illusion of green air. They place a veil between us and the hours of strong afternoon sun. In winter they become sparse enough to let us see the harbor and places west of it, Wamphassuc Point and even Noank spire on a clear day.

It takes me a little while to get worked up to the job, although I already own a lightweight aluminum extension ladder. I call Mr. Browning for permission; he says please go right ahead, cut whatever's bothering you. He had been meaning to do it himself but hadn't got around to it. I have a Swedish bucksaw, a bit dull from cutting the hickory logs I rescued from the town dump. I also have a small Japanese pruning saw—an eighty-nine-cent special from the lumberyard bargain shelf—in case the bucksaw proves unmanageable. Then all I need is someone to hold the ladder. The willows afford no solid spot on which to rest the ladder. They sway, and the top rung slides on the smooth and bending boughs. I hang on with one hand and saw nervously with the other—the nervousness being partly physical, from the act of hanging on and sawing and hoping that the whole works isn't going to tip and topple me off onto the palisade of picket fencing twenty feet below. And it is partly emotional, resulting from the thought that Mr. Browning may suddenly look out and see me up in his trees and change his mind—hey, he really is cutting them back! The act of cutting also contributes to my nervous condition, the act of sawing into the soft green marrow of the bough, which is alive and part of the tree and now slowly bends and breaks. It is often at this point that one's associate seems to catch the nervous contagion and starts to call up: "Do you really think you ought to be cutting that much?" or "Did he *really* say he didn't mind?" And since the act of asking these upsetting questions seems to require my trusty helper to take one or even two hands from the ladder, reaching into a pocket to wipe sweat (caused by embarrassment, surely, rather than effort) from his flushed brow, the ladder begins to wobble. I decide that, anyway, my arm is aching from sawing one-handed. I descend. I say: "I suppose that will do." There is still thick shade over the dahlias, and in a strong westerly breeze the topmost willow branches reach out toward the house, nearly brushing it. But there it is, done until I build up the energy for another session.

I suppose one can read in this a sort of wariness of one's neighbors—a salutary wariness which is generally mirrored by the attitude of the neighbors themselves. We live very close to each other and try not to underline the fact. Yet the neighbors are there when needed, and it is something we bear in mind when we hear that someone from New York would like to buy so-and-so's house for an astronomical sum, which will mean that it will be lived in for three months of the year. Not long after we moved to School Street, Liz—who was then two and a half—got lost. Margot thought she was playing in the garden, but the gate wasn't properly locked, and the next time she looked, Liz had gone. Margot then tried the nearby houses and gardens. She knocked on doors. And pretty soon the women in the neighboring houses who had all said, "No, Liz isn't here," were—without being asked—out looking for her. Some of them walked around the block. Mrs. Cabral got in her big Pontiac and drove around the village. Mrs. Arruda walked to the Point to look on the beach. They called at other houses and telephoned the school. Just when Margot was about to call the police, one of the neighbors brought back word from the bank, at Cannon Square. The manager said a little girl with curly hair had walked into the vault and was playing with the money.

In the village the people we know are of all ages; it is possible—and it is something we think of as one of the great advantages of the place—to know older people well. There are of course plenty of old farts, but there are plenty of young ones too. In a city there tend to be strata of certain ages, subdivided into groups of certain occupations. Here, sympathies of mind and temperament are more important than years and careers. Henry and Paula Chapin, for instance, are among the most congenial people I know. Henry is seventy-six and Paula is seventy. Henry is an excellent gardener, and in season can be seen walking through the village streets with a great basket of eggplant, zucchini, tomatoes, and lettuce, his surplus crop, which he brings to young housewives who take his fancy. Henry has a Viking beard and a timeless glitter in his eyes. As for Paula, his wife and intellectual sparring partner—there are no flies on Paula. She teaches remedial reading to children with dyslexia, which is a problem of seeing words backwards. She has her own garden, with less vegetables than Henry's, more herbs in it. In the course of two winters in Greece she learned demotic Greek and wandered around Thessaly, walking and taking buses. On Wednesday evenings in summer she appears at the starting line of the handicap small-boat races, her silver hair in a tight bun at the back of her neck, one hand on the tiller and the other grasping the mainsheet of her Beetle catboat (which is called *Rosy*). After asking a few questions about the course that confuse the race committee, she concentrates and sails a fast race. Paula is not someone to let things ride when they don't strike her as right. For example, when the local investor-owned utility wouldn't do anything about it, Paula decided to make her own adjustments to the street light outside 52 Main Street. The light shone too brightly into her bedroom and kept her awake. One evening after dinner she got Rust Hills, her son-in-law, to climb a ladder and install a tin shade she had designed for the job—to create a shadow in the quadrant of her window. While he was up the pole, and Paula was standing at the foot, directing operations, the police car came by, and stopped. The patrolman called out: "What are you doing there?"

Paula said: "Officer, my son-in-law is making adjustments to the light so that it doesn't bother me."

The policeman thought a moment, nodded, and drove on.

❦

OUR LIVES are largely made up of eating and sleeping, of getting meals and washing up, of playing hide-and-go-seek with the children or alternately harassing them or encouraging them to do homework, brush their teeth, and go to bed. Time goes in writing letters, taking showers, reading in bed, picking up things that have been dropped all over the house, going to the bank, answering the telephone, waiting for the mailman, paying the newspaper boy, turning away vacuum-cleaner salesmen, watching an hour of television, standing with our arms around each other or, furious, a long way apart. Time is spent writing checks. In Stonington I pay my bills and save postage by taking around the checks myself once a month—the tour consists of Palmer's Gas Station, the Book Mart, the Lumber Company, Bindloss Fuel and Hardware, and the Drug Store. We spend a certain amount of time laughing and some time shouting, and now and then we have moments in which a word or two, hardly a conversation, indicates a mood in common. Sometimes it is an enthusiasm, sometimes a state of depression. I wonder if this dissatisfaction springs from the fact that we don't seem to be changing the world, but are merely holding it together. I think on some days that a greater life is going on elsewhere, that we are in a shallow backwater of the world; but on others I am confident that that "greater" life is of less worth; this is the way the world should be arranged. We should all live in villages.

My neighbor Peter Tripp thinks this is going to happen anyway, as a result of the breakdown of our conglomerate-swollen civilization—he thinks next year will be the great civil war, both ends against the middle, and after that will come the era of the thousand city-states and village-states. We compare prognostications over the garden fence, while he is digging his lettuce patch and I am repairing the jungle gym. Peter's ultimate optimism is based in gloom. Oil in the harbor, state senators boosting a jetport in the woods to the north of us, a country which is car-crazy, car- and oil- and mobility-dominated, and has people running round in it demanding the SST and compulsory sterilization programs—these things make him certain the whole nation is about to come to pieces, lots of little pieces; and that further prospect enchants him. Grass growing on long stretches of the interstate expressway system. A customs and immigration checkpoint at the gate to Stonington village. And maybe somewhere in the impenetrable depths of the

continent a capital, from which ornate powerless pro-
nouncements now and then come forth as in the late
days of the Holy Roman Empire, signed with the com-
puter pictogram of the hereditary President, Spiro the
Thirteenth.

My optimism is differently based. For one thing, it
seems to me that in many ways this country isn't
crowded enough. It is thinly and fluidly peopled. It
needs less development and more settlement, more culti-
vation. Sprawls need centers, and centers need citizens,
not commuters who come and go, not superintendents
who keep an eye on things, but people who belong.
Rather than blow up the conglomerate in a fatal explosion, it might be better to make sure it did a just and
efficient job of what it alone can do, namely, distributing
the losses and profits of all the subsidiaries, some of
which are starving and need help in millions, and some of
which need dietary help in the form of fat being removed, also by the millions. Within the conglomerate
there ought to be plenty of opportunity for "participa-
tion" and "decision-making"—not that a village or
neighborhood needs to control its own foreign policy,
but it does need to look after its own fabric. Scale is the
essential; a certain size for a certain function has to be insisted on. We need to recover the ability to give things—
fire engines, pullman cars—names rather than numbers.
This country remains gripped by the myth that unless
something keeps getting bigger and bigger it is doomed.

In fact, the reverse is often true, as some magazines with millions of circulation are beginning to realize. It may be harder to stay small, but then the growth may be within.

The settlers of the original New England villages had some idea of this. When a village reached a point where it was becoming too big for its institutions—its land and its church—it sent out a group to settle elsewhere, and there have the same respect for the balance between human society and the natural surroundings. A good deal of that respect and that self-control has been lost. But the village preserves the stamp of it. Even if the outline can no longer be precisely copied, the form remains exemplary. And since much of what we find objectionable about the modern state and the modern city is a result of disassociation between man and a place, a result of the various consequences of industrialization (whether slums or suburbs), and since it seems to me that the post-industrial future is going to allow, through improved communications, men to stay at home and work, and read, and grow lettuce, I believe the example will be in demand. Not just for villages as villages, but—like London—cities of villages.

❧ 22 ❧

THERE WAS A TIME when time was sun-time. Days were
framed by the rising and setting of the sun, and divided
with the help of sundials or a noon mark set on the
kitchen windowsill. The first public clock in Connecticut was installed by one Ebenezer Parmelee in Guilford
meetinghouse in 1726. Now, besides the electric clock
over the stove and what the television indicates if we
turn it on, we can get the time from sound as well as
light: the sound of those afternoon papers hitting the
sidewalk outside the Arrudas', the sound of the seven
o'clock or shortly thereafter fire whistle, and the sound
of the Federal, the last night train, hooting for the gate-
less crossings at Walkers Dock and Wamphassuc Point
on its way from Boston to Washington—a sound we
hear more clearly with a northwest to northeasterly
wind.

One characteristic daytime sound of the village is
hammering. I noticed this one spring morning when I'd
gone up on the roof to fix a leak. From three or four
places within earshot came the sound of nails being
banged into wood. There were also sounds of wood

being cut and shaped—the sounds of wooden houses being remodeled, fixed up, and cared for. Down on Hancox Street someone was having a rotten section of gutter removed. On Omega Ed Smith was hanging his new front door. Several carpenters who work for the contractor Donald Palmer were busy on a kitchen extension of a house on Water Street, while on Trumbull Street Tony Previty was installing wooden shingles on one side of his garage. When, shortly after moving in, I built a wooden fence across the entrance to our side yard, my neighbor cast a suspicious eye on it and said that he knew I'd built it myself—it didn't look like a contractor's job, it looked like the work of a handyman. Wooden houses make us handymen.

On the roof I sit with a big can of black roofing compound and an old brush, around whose handle I have wrapped a section torn from an L. L. Bean shirt, whose collar and cuffs decayed some time ago. The compound is a sort of tar. I have worked my way across the fragile, elderly shingles, whose coarse sandpapery surface provides friction for the soles of my boots and the seat of my trousers. I keep my weight low. The chimney and the television antenna furnish handholds as I seek spots where the shingles are worn away, exposing the wood beneath or the rusty heads of old roofing nails. The tar goes on like black treacle; that is, it tends to stay on the spoon rather than be transferred to the porridge, and then, when one seems to have successfully plastered it

on, and one takes away the spoon, a good deal of
porridge comes up too. So as I work across the roof the
tar is applied with a brush clogged with bits and pieces
of old shingle, and pretty soon, when it seems to me that
I am doing more damage to the roof than repair, I climb
to the ridge and rest.

Up here the view of the village is fine. The skyline:
roofs, dormers, antennae, chimneys, water-towers,
church towers, cupolas, and trees. Black roofs, gray
roofs, red roofs, green roofs, and roofs with wooden
shingles, the nicest texture. John Lawrence, my next-
door neighbor, has a roof whose southern slope he has
recently re-covered with green asphalt shingles, but the
northern side, which faces me and is a little less exposed
to weather and sun, is still old wooden shingles, cracked
and worn, and in damp weather covered with a thin film
of green moss. I hope they last forever. McVitty, the architect, has a thing about flat roofs, and on Pat Willson's
new wing, down on Hancox Street, which I can just see
between the Cabrals' and the Arrudas', he has designed a
flat roof covered with gravel, on which small pools of
water collect and in cold weather freeze, forming mir-
rors in which seagulls can see themselves. The high-
pitched roof of the Waldron house is singular in being
corrugated steel. But, in fact, none of the roofs are alike;
two houses side by side and probably built by the same
builder reveal, after a hundred years of accretion and repair, slight differences. On one the main chimney has dis-

appeared; on the other a dormer has been added. The York house has a true widow's walk. The Avellars have a tall cupola with windows on all sides. A few houses have anemometers, with small cups whizzing around, that measure the wind speed. From the chimney at the velvet-mill a tall plume of charcoal-colored smoke shoots up, and bends away on the breeze.

Three towers loom above the village. One is the modified tower of the old Baptist church, now a house—modified, that is, by a former owner, who didn't like the dunce's cap arrangement which used to top it, and re-placed it with a flat deck, railed around. The second is the tower, authentically early-nineteenth-century, of the Congregational church. And the third is the tower-turning-into-spire of the new Catholic church. Like an expensive plastic flower, it looks tremendous from a dis-tance but corny and imitative from close-up. In the tower of the old Baptist church there is a double bed suspended by four chains. The present owners say it makes them seasick. In the tower of the Congregational church is a clock, usually four minutes slow. The Catho-lic belfry contains electronic chimes.

The town hall has taken over some of the political function the church used to have as a meetinghouse. Moreover, although there is bingo at St. Mary's, ham and bean suppers at the United Congregational-Baptist, and gourmet lunches, served by the Churchwomen's Guild, at Calvary Episcopal (sometimes preceded by a

talk and discussion on current affairs—for example, the
Arab-Israeli crisis), the churches have a secular rival:
the Community Center. It has a new building, a low,
brick, four-hundred-thousand-dollar edifice designed in
Greater A & P or savings-bank-Colonial style. It is situated on the edge of the marsh, on the north side of the
viaduct, behind Al Palmer's gas station. (Critics of its
cost and architecture claim that it is already settling at
either end into the marsh. However, this may be an opti-
cal illusion created by the shape of the building, height-
ened by air-conditioning machinery amidships, and the
shape of the mound it is built on. On the other hand, it is
said that Al Palmer has to have his garage jacked up
every year or so in order that masons can pour in, under
the foundations, more fill and concrete.) The community center is in some respects an expression of the pre-
vailing belief that children, specifically teenage children,
get into trouble unless they are kept physically active.
The more prosperous village residents are prepared to
put good money into keeping them so. Basketball is one
good answer. There are also dances at the "Como" on
Saturday nights, ski trips, and swimming programs. An
ex-army officer, Frank Turek, runs everything, an
unsung hero, the organizing power behind every scene.
For other age groups, there's a nursery school for tots
and toddlers, modern dance and ceramic classes for
young mothers, and a television lounge for the so-called
golden agers. The structure is there if anyone comes up

with some good ideas for mind- or spirit-stirring stimulus to affect us between the cradle and the grave.

In the skyline, trees splay their tall fans, bony and gray still at this time of year, though here and there with a nascent touch of green. Trees, made by God and planted by the Village Improvement Association, take in moisture, absorb gasoline fumes, provide humus for the soil, and break the wind. It seems a special bonus that they are also beautiful. Between the trees are all the wires and cables strung by telephone and electricity companies. Is it comforting to know that Stonington had an anti-telephone pole movement in 1895 when they first appeared? Now the poles dominate the streets, and are every year festooned with thicker wires and more equipment: junction boxes, transformers, power lines, and—soon—TV cables. I keep track of the number of wires that are draped in front of our bedroom window, between us and our second-floor view of Sandy Point. I am ready to squawk if they hang one more. But most people are used to them, and a few find them so much a part of the visual scene—like fences and sidewalks—that they would miss them if, with the new sewer pipes, the wires were put underground.

Fences, at least, have a variety in the village that the poles lack. Between the Arcade building and the bank there is a splendid white wooden fence topped with a high green hedge. There are ornate iron fences outside the Dunnings and the Culbert Palmers. Grace Stone has a plain wooden fence whose simplicity always attracts me, while across the street from her the Baums are surrounded by fancy gingerbread fretwork. A few unfeeling people have put up frontier-type wooden stockades through and over which one can't see. One makes up for it by asking: What do you think they're doing behind there?

In a few places in the village you can still see poking through later coatings of asphalt the stones, the stepping stones, which formed pedestrian street crossings only fifty or sixty years ago when streets were still mostly dirt and in winter often muddy. I have a photograph of the Fourth of July parade taken eight years ago. It already looks antique. The reason—I decided after a few minutes of looking at it—was that since I took the picture the light-colored, cracked concrete surface of Water Street has been paved with a smooth layer of black tar. The street surfaces are now like that throughout the village, but the sidewalks still reflect the fact that they are the responsibility though not the possession of the householders whose frontage they cross. When walking, I notice the variety of sidewalks. The stone paving slabs on the west side of Wadawanuck Square are slippery after rain, and especially so if leaves have fallen on them, or the seeds have dropped from the overhanging maple trees. In front of the Knoxes' house on the other side of the square the sidewalk is a sort of terrace cut into the bank. The pocked and broken sidewalk outside one mansion on Main Street accurately portrays the antisocial character of the owner—or so people feel who have twisted an ankle in one of the crevices. There are no brick sidewalks, though several houses have nicely considered brick paths leading to their back doors; and in a few places, as on Broad Street going down toward Gold Street, there are no sidewalks at all, merely a grass verge on which feet have worn a track. One or two curbstones still have rings and eye-bolts let into them for horses and carriages. Outside the Baums there's an upping stone, on which ladies could climb two stone steps to mount their horses. Opposite Calvary church a long dry-stone wall demonstrates what the settlers found on the land here, and why—when naming the village—they named it Stonington. Like most words, it sounds hollow and strange when you repeat it, but it suits the place, and is fulfilled by the life and lives we invest in it.

A NOTE ABOUT THE AUTHOR

ANTHONY BAILEY is the author of four other nonfiction books: *The Light in Holland* (1970), *The Thousand Dollar Yacht* (1968), *Through the Great City* (1967), and *The Inside Passage* (1965), as well as two novels, *The Mother Tongue* (1961) and *Making Progress* (1959). He is a staff writer for *The New Yorker*; his work has also appeared in magazines on both sides of the Atlantic: in *Horizon, Holiday*, and *The New York Times Magazine* in this country, and in *The Observer, New Statesman,* and *The Times* in England.

Mr. Bailey was born in England in 1933 and was educated at Oxford. He now lives in Stonington, Connecticut, with his wife and four daughters.

A NOTE ON THE TYPE

THE TEXT of this book was set on the Linotype in Janson, a recutting made direct from type cast from matrices long thought to have been made by the Dutchman Anton Janson, who was a practicing type founder in Leipzig during the years 1668–87. However, it has been conclusively demonstrated that these types are actually the work of Nicholas Kis (1650–1702), a Hungarian, who most probably learned his trade from the master Dutch type founder Dirk Voskens. The type is an excellent example of the influential and sturdy Dutch types that prevailed in England up to the time William Caslon developed his own incomparable designs from these Dutch faces.

Composed, printed and bound by The Colonial Press Inc., Clinton, Mass.

Typography and binding design by Virginia Tan